Frankenstein
Teacher's Guide and Lesson Activities
Common Core State Standards Aligned
Revised Edition

by

Elizabeth Chapin-Pinotti

Did I request thee, Maker, from my clay
To mould me man? Did I solicit thee
From darkness to promote me?

John Milton's *Paradise Lost*

ISBN-13: 978-0692268742 (Lucky Willy Publishing)

ISBN-10: 069226874X

© Lucky Willy Publishing. Elizabeth Chapin-Pinotti. All rights reserved.   No part of this publication can be reproduced or transmitted in any form or by anyone except for the classroom use of the person who purchased this curriculum. Any other reproduction is strictly prohibited. Lucky Willy Publishing is a division of Lucky Jenny Publishing. Plymouth, California.

www.luckyjenny.com

Table of Contents

Discussion Question 1: *Who is the actual monster in* Frankenstein *and why?*

Discussion Question 2: *What responsibility did Victor, and the creator, have towards the monster?*

Discussion Question 3: *Victor warns Robert that acquiring knowledge can lead to "destruction and infallible misery". What serious consequences may the acquisition of knowledge have?*

Discussion Question 4: *Scholars often use* Frankenstein *is an argument against scientific technological advancement and knowledge acquisition that creates life forms; others argument that it is not technology itself but how technology is used that presents ethical dilemmas. What is Shelley's position? What is your position?*

Discussion Question 5: *How do gender roles play a role in the theme of* Frankenstein*? Do the characters have traditional gender roles? In what way does the novel break away and reverse the same gender roles?*

Discussion Question 6: *How is the pursuit of knowledge and scientific discovery portrayed in the novel? Is the pursuit of knowledge seen as a positive or a negative force? Why?*

Discussion Question 7: *What character in the novel has the best moral compass and why?*

Socratic Seminar Participant Rubric

"I do know that for the sympathy of one living being, I would make peace with all. I have love in me the likes of which you can scarcely imagine and rage the likes of which you would not believe. If I cannot satisfy the one, I will indulge the other."

— Mary Shelley, *Frankenstein*

Teacher Page: Elements of the Gothic Novel

Frankenstein; or, The Modern Prometheus by Mary Shelley was published anonymously in London in 1818. Written in the summer of 1816, when Mary Shelley and her future husband poet Percy Shelley were visiting Lord Byron in Geneva, Frankenstein is often called the first science fiction novel. In Shelley's fateful tale, Victor Frankenstein animates a creature from various dismembered corpses. The creature is enormous and physically hideous and thus cruelly cast aside by his creator, left to wander the countryside, seeking companionship and eventually revenge, as he grows increasingly knowledgeable, brutal and destructive.

The story came to be during that rainy summer on a bet. Mary, her husband, Lord Byron, and Lord Byron's physician and friend John Polidori, spent many hours that year reading German ghost stories. At one point, Byron suggested they have a contest to see who could write the best "ghost" story of their own– and Frankenstein was born. The novel was part of the Romantic Movement and is Gothic in style. Sub-titled *The Modern Prometheus,* it serves as a warning against man playing God by overreaching scientifically; it also serves as a reflection of the effects of the Industrial Revolution firmly taking hold.

NOTE: In Greek mythology Prometheus is a Titan who "created man from clay". This Titan also stole fire for human use – thus enabling progress and civilization. Prometheus was punished as a result of this theft. Zeus, the king of the gods, sentenced Prometheus to an eternity bound to a rock and each day an eagle was to feed on his liver, which would grow back so the bird could feed again the next day. Prometheus is a figure that represents the human reach for scientific knowledge, the risk of overreaching and the unintended consequences thereof.[1] It is interesting to note that Percy Shelley wrote a lyrical drama in 1820 titled *Prometheus Unbound* and some researchers suggest that Shelley had a hand in the writing of Frankenstein as Mary was only 19-years-old at the time it was penned. Professor Charles Robinson, of the University of Delaware, combed the original manuscript and found many additions and deletions in Percy Shelley's handwriting. Professor Robinson believes the book should be credited: "by Mary Shelley with Percy Shelley". Indeed, Robinson found some 5,000 changes to a pre-publication copy. Robinson published this version of the classic – sans Percy's comments. (*The Original Frankenstein*, Vintage Classics).

A Bit of History: The Goths were a Germanic tribe who fought against the Holy Roman Empire for many decades. The Goths reached the height of their power around the 5th century A.D. During the Renaissance "gothic" came to describe architecture and art built during the Middle Ages. More time passed and "gothic" became a term applied to novels set in Gothic-style architecture – abbeys and castles and such. Think scenes of hell and gargoyles carved on cathedrals and decaying mansions – and the idea of the Gothic novel takes form.

The Gothic-style novel was part of the Romantic Movement in literature; however the relatively more casual style (when compared to the standard "Romantic Movement" novel) seems to react against the formalness of most Romantic literature.

The Romantic Movement was rife with disenfranchised liberals who sought solitude in nature. They believed emotional healing could be found in the natural world and thus imagery surrounding nature became a prominent feature of Romantic literature.

The theme of "disenfranchised man" is very common. Said man, finds himself unable to live in society and is often sympathized with or even revered. Frankenstein and the monster are both disenfranchised – the monster

---

1. William Hansen, *Classical Mythology: A Guide to the Mythical World of the Greeks and Romans* (Oxford University Press, 2005), pp. 32, 48–50, 69–73, 93, 96, 102–104, 140; as trickster figure, p. 310 and Lewis Richard Farnell, *The Cults of the Greek States* (Oxford: Clarendon Press, 1896), vol. 1, pp. 36, 49, 75, 277, 285, 314, 346; Carol Dougherty, *Prometheus* (Routledge, 2006), p. 42ff.

because his hideous form keeps him from the compassion and companionship of others and Victor because of his inadvertent self-imposed isolation after creating the monster. As the novel progresses, Victor becomes withdrawn, emaciated and unable to enjoy the company of others. In Frankenstein, Shelley almost creates two sides of the same being in the characters of the monster and Victor – as each ascends and transcends into isolation, revenge, despair and ultimately demise.

Many Romantic writers deal with the supernatural – as is the case in Mary Shelley's Frankenstein. In this novel, romantic notions take the ordinary and make it extraordinary. The Gothic novel within the Romantic Movement brought with it the notion of adding things, not possible in real life, to literature. Whereas, previous fiction had more of a realistic feel, the Gothic novel borders fantasy. Creating life, in a lab, using decaying parts of other beings, was not a realistic fixture in the 1810s and the cognitive reasoning developed by the monster has been alluded to as one of the first examples of science fiction.

The Gothic world is the fallen world, both literally and figuratively and Gothic novels often contain either an element of impending doom, revenge or superstition. The fall is often brought on by the deeds of an ancestor – like in The Fall of the House of Usher or brought on by a character playing God as in Frankenstein – as Victor uses science to create a being.

The setting of a Gothic novel is dark and foreboding – creating an atmosphere of horror and decay. Characters may include supernatural entities and/or beings fallen from grace. Gothic plots often contain hidden secrets or mysteries that must be sorted through. Gothic novels are dark, symbolically and literally, with weather used to cast a foreboding tone.

Gothic Characters: In Gothic literature the protagonist is alone and often an archetype. The isolation can be literal or emotional. In Frankenstein it is both. Frankenstein consistently imposes isolation upon himself – for example, when creating the monster, Victor locks himself away, when he returns home to Geneva and is locked out of the gates of the city, when he locks himself away again to create the monster's requested mate and then, at the end of the novel, when he journeys to find the monster he is alone until he meets up with Walton. This isolation can be self-imposed or as a result of circumstances.

Both Victor and the monster are emotionally alone. *"I am alone and miserable; man will not associate with me; but one as deformed and horrible as myself would not deny herself to me. My companion must be of the same species and have the same defects. This being you must create."* (Chapter 16 the monster).

Women are usually characterized subserviently – as damsels in distress – helpless and in need of rescue. Emotions and passions run high in Gothic literature. The antagonist is evil or a sinner or embodies temptation. There are often ghostly or supernatural characters: think werewolves, vampires and witches – or created monsters such as in Frankenstein.

Important: This is a cool novel and students should be allowed to experience this coolness. It is ironic how Frankenstein is usually taught in AP or Honors courses – which is fine – but the content and the background are ripe for alternative education as well! Frankenstein poses a tremendous opportunity to hook students on reading. The content is epic and the back-story on how and where the book was written is intriguing and even relatable to students who normally shun literature. A great edition for struggling readers or at-risk students is the Vintage Classics edition, The Original Frankenstein. In this version, Professor Charles Robinson worked from the original surviving draft, often omitting Percy Shelley's notes, as well as decades of revisions. Mary Shelley's words harbor a directness lacking in Percy's poetic prose – which makes for a more modern and easier read for most students.

Talking about how the novel was conceived will intrigue most students – so share it with them! Acknowledge how old Mary Shelley was when she wrote her book, talk about her background and how she was unmarried when she accompanied the older Percy Shelley to Lord Byron's house on Lake Geneva. Talk about how the novel was written as a bet – to see who could write the best ghost story. There is an abundance of material on this subject – ripe for sharing with students. Make your lessons juicy and students will eat them up!!! That said – there are a couple of amazing other versions out there:

One Summer in Geneva 1816: This edition talks about the conception of Frankenstein and contains literacy non-fiction reading for the Common Core State Standards. This volume also includes the work of another author and visitor of Lord Byron's, during that infamous summer, who wrote his story for the same bet or competition: John Politori's The Vampyre as well as and excerpt from The Life and Letters of Mary Wollstonecraft Shelley by Julian Marshall and selected letters that can be analyzed as source documents.

This version tells how… "In 1816 Mary Godwin (Shelley) and poet-philosopher Percy Shelley traveled to Geneva, Switzerland to spend the summer with their friend Lord Byron. They whiled away their time on the waterfront boating, writing and talking late into many summer nights. This was the summer in which Frankenstein was conceived. Research suggests that Mary, Percy, Lord Byron and Byron's guest, physician and writer, John Polidori, decided, at the suggestion of Lord Byron, to have a competition to see who could write the best supernatural story. It seems the summer was rainy and the group spent many hours amusing themselves reading German ghost stories and were thusly inspired. Shortly thereafter Mary Godwin had a waking dream and Frankenstein was born. Mary was 19-years-old. Also, born of the same competition was the most famous of John Polidori's works: The Vampyre. This story was originally credited to Lord Byron; however, both he and Polidori attested it was indeed conceived and written by Polidori. **Contained within this publication**: Mary Shelley's Frankenstein, John Polidori's The Vampyre plus an excerpt from The Life and Letters of Mary Wollstonecraft Shelley by Julian Marshall and an excerpt from the Selected English Letters (XV-XIX) arranged by M. Duckitt and H. Wragg (1913)."

- **ISBN-10:** 0615824951
- **ISBN-13:** 978-0615824956

The Original Frankenstein: "Working from the earliest surviving draft of Frankenstein, Charles E. Robinson presents two versions of the classic novel—as Mary Shelley originally wrote it and a subsequent version clearly indicating Percy Shelley's amendments and contributions.

For the first time we can hear Mary's sole voice, which is colloquial, fast-paced, and sounds more modern to a contemporary reader. We can also see for the first time the extent of Percy Shelley's contribution—some 5,000 words out of 72,000—and his stylistic and thematic changes. His occasionally florid prose is in marked contrast to the directness of Mary's writing. Interesting, too, are Percy's suggestions, which humanize the monster, thus shaping many of the major themes of the novel as we read it today. In these two versions of Frankenstein we have an exciting new view of one of literature's greatest works.

- **ISBN-10:** 0307474429
- **ISBN-13:** 978-0307474421

Common Core State Standard 11-12 RL. 1: Cite strong and thorough textual evidence to support analysis of what the text says explicitly as well as inferences drawn from the text, including determining where the text leaves matters uncertain. *This standard is evident here and in each of the sets of Comprehension questions.*

Frankenstein Themes: Universal Ideas explored through literary work

Objective for Common Core Standard 11-12 RL. 2: Theme 2.1: Determine two or more themes in literature and analyze their development.

Teacher Notes: Theme plays an imperative role when we analyze the questions raised or explored within the meaning of a text – besides the literal words. Make sure students understand that a theme is the underlying meaning of a literary work and that a theme may be either stated or implied. Rich works of literature usually have many themes. Four of those found within <u>Frankenstein</u> are listed below. Please note, there are others.

- **Theme 1:** Pursuit of knowledge or ignorance is bliss. Briefly discuss this theme as it relates to the novel, pair up students and ask them to re-read the example of theme 1 provided and then search for other examples within the novel. Alone or in pairs, have students answer the associated prompt. Repeat for each theme
- **Theme 2:** Shroud of Secrecy
- **Theme 3:** Man's inhumanity to those who are different
- **Theme 4:** Feminism

Interpreting themes is part creativity and part skill and, as long as one supports his or her analysis with real evidence from the literature, one may discover themes anew. There is not one answer to what is the theme of a particular work. It is all a matter of interpretation and then using critical evidence to back up one's assertions.

Again, students must understand that, on the most base level, a theme is the underlying meaning of a literary work. A theme may be stated or implied.

Theme Activity 1: Ignorance or Bliss/Pursuit of Knowledge

Read and discuss.

Theme 1: Ignorance is bliss or the pursuit of knowledge. In 1816, when Frankenstein was written, reasoning and thinking through the science and technology of the day challenged many established "truths" about the world and man's relationship to God as the creator. At the same time, these "truths" were being questioned as science and technology stressed the limits of human capacity. Shelley inserts the counter-humanist notions, for example, in Chapter 4 when Victor warms Walton :

> *I see by your eagerness and the wonder and hope which your eyes express, my friend, that you expect to be informed of the secret with which I am acquainted; that cannot be; listen patiently until the end of my story, and you will easily perceive why I am reserved upon that subject. I will not lead you on, unguarded and ardent as I then was, to your destruction and **infallible** misery. Learn from me, if not by my precepts, at least by my example, how dangerous is the acquirement of knowledge and how much happier that man is who believes his native town to be the world, than he who aspires to become greater than his nature will allow.*

> *When I found so astonishing a power placed within my hands, I hesitated a long time concerning the manner in which I should employ it. Although I possessed the capacity of bestowing animation, yet to prepare a frame for the reception of it, with all its intricacies of fibers, muscles, and veins, still remained a work of **inconceivable** difficulty and labor. I doubted at first whether I should attempt the creation of a being like myself, or one of simpler organization; but my imagination was too much exalted by my first success to permit me to doubt of my ability to give life to an animal as complex and wonderful as man.*

In this passage, Shelley seems to wonder, through her characters, if some things are better left alone. If perhaps there should be limits on what man knows. Likewise, the alternative title of the book The Modern Prometheus espouses this theme. Note: Prometheus was a Greek mythological figure who took fire from the gods, gave it to man and then suffered the consequences.

In a similar way, Victor is giving life to a being – something that was reserved for the creator in 1816. He is stealing God's idea, like Prometheus, and gifting it to humans. Prometheus' suffering foreshadows Victor's destiny. Victor is attempting to reach beyond the limits of humanity into the realm most believed should not be entered and with that will/should come consequences.

This pursuit of knowledge eventually drives Victor to his death. He loathes the monster he's created. Walton similarly attempts to reach beyond and travel to the great North; however he pulls back learning from Victor how destructive the search for knowledge can be. This transitions into Theme 2.

This first theme is introduced from Walton's very first letters when the stranger tells Walton – *"you seek for knowledge and wisdom, as I once did; and I ardently hope that the gratification of your wishes may not be a serpent to sting you, as mine has been."*

From the beginning, Walton demonstrates his intrigue with the opportunity to know what no one else knows and to uncover the secrets of nature. *"What may not be expected in a country of eternal light?"*

Examples of Theme 1 – Ignorance is bliss or the pursuit of knowledge:

- **Chapter 4,** Victor: *Learn from me, if not by my precepts, at least by my example, how dangerous is the acquirement of knowledge and how much happier that man is who believes his native town to be the world, than he who aspires to become greater than his nature will allow.*

- **Chapter 5,** Victor: *The different accidents of life are not so changeable as the feelings of human nature. I had worked hard for nearly two years, for the sole purpose of infusing life into an inanimate body. For this I had deprived myself of rest and health. I had desired it with an ardour that far exceeded moderation; but now that I had finished, the beauty of the dream vanished, and breathless horror and disgust filled my heart. Unable to endure the aspect of the being I had created, I rushed out of the room and continued a long time traversing my bed-chamber, unable to compose my mind to sleep.*

- **Chapter 20,** Victor: *Even if they were to leave Europe and inhabit the deserts of the new world, yet one of the first results of those sympathies for which the daemon thirsted would be children, and a race of devils would be propagated upon the earth who might make the very existence of the species of man a condition precarious and full of terror. Had I right, for my own benefit, to inflict this curse upon everlasting generations? I had before been moved by the sophisms of the being I had created; I had been struck senseless by his fiendish threats; but now, for the first time, the wickedness of my promise burst upon me; I shuddered to think that future ages might curse me as their pest, whose selfishness had not hesitated to buy its own peace at the price, perhaps, of the existence of the whole human race.*

- **Chapter 21,** Victor: *To me the walls of a dungeon or a palace were alike hateful. The cup of life was poisoned forever, and although the sun shone upon me, as upon the happy and gay of heart, I saw around me nothing but a dense and frightful darkness...*

Teacher Notes:

Name(s): _____ Date: _____

1. Site Example of Theme 1: Ignorance is bliss or pursuit of knowledge. _____

_____
_____
_____
_____
_____
_____
_____
_____

2. Elaborate on how the passage above relates to the this theme. _____

_____
_____
_____
_____
_____
_____
_____
_____

3. Discuss an example in your life when you have been affected by the tenets of this theme. _____

_____
_____
_____
_____
_____
_____
_____
_____

4. Compare and contrast your experience with this theme to that of the character affected in your chosen passage.

Passage   Both   My Experience

Theme Activity 2: Shroud of Secrecy

Theme 2: Shroud of Secrecy: Through Victor, science is a mystery that must be unveiled; however, once unveiled, the knowledge gathered must be kept secret. In the passage below (Chapter 3) Victor considers M. Krempe contemptible but an excellent scientist because he is "deeply imbued in the ***secrets of science***".

Victor's obsession with creating life is veiled in secrecy – even to the point of risking the life of Justine and waiting until their wedding night to disclose his secret to Elizabeth. Victor reveals his plans and actions to no one until that time. His obsession becomes so absorbing that he even stops visiting his friends and loved ones. The monster harbors his own secrets, mostly due to the fact that his appearance has forced him into seclusion.

Walton is truth and serves as such in his "narrative". Through Walton, Victor escapes the secrets that have ruined his life, while the monster forges a human connection to Walton.

*The next morning I delivered my letters of introduction and paid a visit to some of the principal professors. Chance—or rather the evil influence, the Angel of Destruction, which asserted omnipotent sway over me from the moment I turned my reluctant steps from my father's door—led me first to M. Krempe, professor of natural philosophy. He was an uncouth man, but deeply imbued in the secrets of his science. He asked me several questions concerning my progress in the different branches of science **appertaining** to natural philosophy.*

This obsession with secrecy proves destructive and corruptive for Victor.

Questions:

1. Analyze the following statement: *The veil of secrecy woven by Victor leads to the death of William.*

_____

_____

_____

_____

_____

_____

_____

2. How does this theme relate to Elizabeth? Specifically elaborate upon the following quote: *"I have one secret, Elizabeth, a dreadful one; when revealed to you, it will chill your frame with horror. I will confide this tale of misery and terror to you the day after our marriage shall take place".*

_____

_____

_____

_____

_____

_____

_____

_____

_____

_____

_____

_____

_____

_____

Theme Activity 3: Real world tie-in.

Common Core State Standards: 11-12. W.2: Objective: Introduce a topic and organize the ideas that support the topic. **Specifically:** You are expected to build new elements on ones that precede them to create a unified hold among information and concepts.

Common Core State Standards: 11-12. SL.1. d: Objective: Respond thoughtfully, synthesize points of an argument and determine additional information that is necessary.

The Price of Secrecy

Victor Frankenstein values secrecy. The one redeeming quality he finds in M. Kempt is that the professor is infused with the secrets of science. Victor himself has a horrific secret of science in that he has tempted nature and created a grotesque being and then, when the being escapes, fails to reveal the danger now eminent to the people around him. When the escape leads to the death of William and the conviction and subsequence hanging of an innocent girl – Victor remains silent. Victor is now alone in his scientific secrecy.

What about scientists today? Do scientists still work under a veil of secrecy, revealing only portions of their research and findings? Are any such secrets being kept today harmful to humanity? Think about some of the issues that have been revealed in the past, scientific secrets that have caused great harm – yet if said secrets had surfaced, lives could have been saved, or in the very least, made a little better.

One example lies within the tobacco industry. In 1994, leading tobacco companies attested to Congress that nicotine was not addictive, even though tobacco industry scientists knew nicotine was addictive because they had been performing extensive studies on the topic since 1964. For thirty years, the secret was kept and even denounced. Think how this secret, and the subsequent lies around it, have affected life and humanity.

Activity: Think of a popular scientific topic you have heard about on the news or have read about on the Internet. Think about what kinds of secrets could eventually arise around your topic and how these secrets could affect life and humanity. Research your topic and summarize any secrets or potential secrets below.

Topic examples include: genetics, fracking, nuclear power or cancer – just to name a few.

Topic: _____

Websites used:

_____
_____
_____

List controversy or potential controversies:

_____
_____
_____
_____
_____
_____
_____
_____
_____

List motive for secrecy:

_____
_____
_____
_____
_____
_____
_____

Analyze research and secrets:

_____
_____
_____
_____
_____
_____
_____
_____
_____
_____
_____
_____
_____
_____
_____
_____
_____
_____
_____
_____
_____
_____
_____
_____
_____
_____
_____
_____
_____
_____
_____
_____
_____
_____
_____

Theme 3: Activity 4

Theme 3: Man's inhumanity to those who are different. Throughout the novel, Frankenstein contemplates this notion. The monster is indeed different, he is an outcast and doesn't belong to society and is thus alienated; however, he desires a companion and seeks revenge on his creator.

His creator, Victor, becomes increasingly like the monster. They both live isolated from society, literally and figuratively, and are miserable – hating life. Through this theme Shelley casts a blain shadow on man's relationship to those deemed as outsiders.

Activity: Select a passage from the novel that expresses man's cruelty or inhumanity to those who are different. Think about a time in your life when you've felt like an outsider. Describe the situation, what you did, what others did to you and compare it to your chosen passage.

_____
_____
_____
_____
_____
_____
_____
_____
_____
_____
_____
_____
_____
_____
_____
_____
_____
_____
_____
_____
_____
_____
_____
_____
_____
_____
_____
_____
_____
_____
_____
_____
_____
_____

Theme 4: Activity 5

Theme 4: A very subtle, but important theme in <u>Frankenstein</u>, is feminism. Throughout the story, Victor alludes to woman as weak and subservient human beings. He emphasizes that women live for and rely on men. The monster, on the other hand, believes that men and women are equal. Victor, the accepted and normal member of society, sees woman as inferior. Victor is a reflection of popular belief. The monster's views mirror the author's more than Victor's do; likewise, the monster's desire for a companion of the opposite sex is not so he can rule over or be superior to her, but so that he may have an equal companion.

In 1792, Mary Shelley's mother, Mary Wollstonecraft, wrote one of the first treatises of feminist philosophy. In <u>Vindication of the Rights of Woman</u>, Wollstonecraft answers the educational and political theorists of her time – those who believe that woman should not have an education or be equal in social stature to their mail counterparts. Wollstonecraft purports that a woman needs an education equal to that of her standing in society so that she can educate her children and be a companion to her husband – rather than just a wife. Wollstonecraft also maintains that woman are not arm candy or chattel but human beings deserving of the same fundamental rights as men.

Mary Shelley grew up reading her mother's words. She believed that all humans have worth. Her mother's <u>Vindication of the Rights of Woman</u> is considered a landmark of Romantic humanist thought. Not only is Wollstonecraft's work evident in how woman are portrayed in <u>Frankenstein</u>, but in the out-casted monster as well.

Activity: Read the following quotes and compare them to the themes of <u>Frankenstein</u>:

- *"Taught from their infancy that beauty is woman's scepter, the mind shapes itself to the body, and roaming round its gilt cage, only seeks to adorn its prison."* Mary Wollstonecraft, <u>A Vindication of the Rights of Woman</u>. **Question:** How does this quote relate to the monster's isolation? Site examples from the novel.
- *"It is vain to expect virtue from women till they are in some degree independent of men."* **Question:** This quote could easily read: *It is vain to expect virtue from the monster until he is independent from his creator"*. Discuss.
- *"Make them free, and they will quickly become wise and virtuous, as men become more so; for the improvement must be mutual, or the injustice which one half of the human race are obligated to submit to, retorting on their oppressors, the virtue of men will be worm-eaten by the insects whom he keeps under his feet"*. Discuss this quote in relation to how Victor feels about woman.

_____
_____
_____
_____
_____
_____
_____
_____
_____
_____
_____
_____
_____

Activity: Socratic Discussion/Seminar

Common Core Anchor Standards Addressed: R1, R2, R5, W1, W9, SL1 and SL4
Teacher Page:
Socratic Discussion/Seminar

A Socratic Seminar is a structured discussion that allows students to engage and disagree in a way that is polite, focused and respectful. This activity enables students to think critically about texts and build confidence in their ideas and thought processes. The discussions that take place within the Socratic Seminar help students analyze, synthesize and evaluate the written word.

Students begin a Socratic Seminar with a list of teacher (or student – depending on the level) generated questions that help the group think critically about the text they are reading. Students pose questions to the group and take turns speaking and listening to each other's thoughts and ideas. All members of the discussion share learning as students work together to gain a deeper understanding of text – as they extend, clarify and challenge themselves and each other.

Hint: Before you begin this activity, develop a signal to politely stop any student who may be dominating the conversation.

1: Students should complete an **Investigative Clarifier** so they truly understand the text.

2: Guide each student to complete the Seminar Template directly following this section. This can be done in class or completed as homework.

3: Break into groups – or circle up one group with leftover students acting as scribes.

4: Establish the rules and norms of the discussion.

5: Review the purpose of the Socratic Seminar and your expectations. Model how students should participate and behave.

6: Select a discussion leader.

7: Set time limit – 30 to 40 minutes is sufficient.

8: Begin the discussion.

9: Debrief – include discussing the group's strengths and weaknesses.

Helpful hints: If your class is large, divide students into two circles – one inner and one outer. Leave one chair in the inner circle empty. This is the "roving seat". Students who are in the inner circle are active discussion members. Students in the outer circle can pop in! If it is not the first time you are doing this activity – you can actually have two Seminars going at the same time. Twenty is about the limit for active participation to be effective for all students; however, students are more engaged if the group size is closer to twelve.

It is imperative to stress that students must reference the text often and that thinking out of the box and analyzing out of the box are essential, and encouraged, for this activity. Teachers should stay out of the conversation, but guide if necessary.

Name: _____ Date: _____

Socratic Seminar Template: <u>Frankenstein</u> by Mary Shelley

Discussion Question:

Who is the actual monster in <u>Frankenstein</u> and why?

Site two main ideas or claims from the novel to support your argument as it relates to the question.

1. _____
_____
_____
_____
_____
_____
_____
_____page:

2. _____
_____
_____
_____
_____
_____
_____
_____page:

List examples SUPPORTING your argument:
_____
_____
_____
_____
_____
_____
_____
_____
_____
_____
_____
_____
_____
_____
_____
_____
_____
_____
_____
_____pages:

List examples COUNTERING your argument:
_____
_____
_____
_____
_____
_____
_____
_____
_____
_____
_____
_____
_____
_____
_____
_____
_____
_____
_____
_____pages:

Name: _____ Date: _____

Socratic Seminar Template: <u>Frankenstein</u> by Mary Shelley

Discussion Question:

What responsibilities did Victor, as the creator, have to the monster?

Site two main ideas or claims from the novel to support your argument as it relates to the question.

1. _____
_____
_____
_____
_____
_____
_____
_____page:

2. _____
_____
_____
_____
_____
_____
_____
_____page:

List examples SUPPORTING your argument:
_____
_____
_____
_____
_____
_____
_____
_____
_____
_____
_____
_____
_____
_____
_____
_____
_____
_____pages:

List examples COUNTERING your argument:
_____
_____
_____
_____
_____
_____
_____
_____
_____
_____
_____
_____
_____
_____
_____
_____
_____
_____pages:

Name: _____ Date: _____

Socratic Seminar Template: <u>Frankenstein</u> by Mary Shelley

Discussion Question:

Victor warns Robert that acquiring knowledge can lead to "destruction and infallible misery". What serious consequences may the acquisition of knowledge have?

Site two main ideas or claims from the novel to support your argument as it relates to the question.

1. _____
   _____
   _____
   _____
   _____
   _____
   _____
   _____page:

2. _____
   _____
   _____
   _____
   _____
   _____
   _____
   _____page:

List examples SUPPORTING your argument:
   _____
   _____
   _____
   _____
   _____
   _____
   _____
   _____
   _____
   _____
   _____
   _____
   _____
   _____
   _____
   _____
   _____pages:

List examples COUNTERING your argument:
   _____
   _____
   _____
   _____
   _____
   _____
   _____
   _____
   _____
   _____
   _____
   _____
   _____
   _____
   _____
   _____pages:

Name: _____ Date: _____

Socratic Seminar Template: <u>Frankenstein</u> by Mary Shelley

Discussion Question:

Scholars often use <u>Frankenstein</u> as an argument against scientific technological advancement and knowledge acquisition that creates life forms; others argue that it is not technology itself but how it is used that presents ethical dilemmas. What is Shelley's position? What is your position?

Site two main ideas or claims from the novel to support your argument as it relates to the question.

1. _____
_____
_____
_____
_____
_____
_____
_____page:

2. _____
_____
_____
_____
_____
_____
_____
_____page:

List examples SUPPORTING your argument:
_____
_____
_____
_____
_____
_____
_____
_____
_____
_____
_____
_____
_____
_____
_____
_____
_____
_____
_____pages:

List examples COUNTERING your argument:
_____
_____
_____
_____
_____
_____
_____
_____
_____
_____
_____
_____
_____
_____
_____
_____
_____
_____pages:

Name: _____ Date: _____

Socratic Seminar Template – Higher Order: <u>Frankenstein</u> by Mary Shelley

Discussion Question:

How do gender roles play a role in the theme of <u>Frankenstein</u>? Do the characters have traditional gender roles? In what way does the novel break away and reverse the same gender roles?

Site two main ideas or claims from the novel to support your argument as it relates to the question.

1. _____
_____
_____
_____
_____
_____
_____page:

2. _____
_____
_____
_____
_____
_____
_____page:

List examples SUPPORTING your argument:
_____
_____
_____
_____
_____
_____
_____
_____
_____
_____
_____
_____
_____
_____
_____
_____
_____
_____pages:

List examples COUNTERING your argument:
_____
_____
_____
_____
_____
_____
_____
_____
_____
_____
_____
_____
_____
_____
_____
_____
_____
_____pages:

Name: _____ Date: _____

Socratic Seminar Template – Higher Order: <u>Frankenstein</u> by Mary Shelley

Discussion Question:

How is the pursuit of knowledge and scientific discovery portrayed in the novel? Is the pursuit of knowledge seen as a positive or a negative force? Why?

Site two main ideas or claims from the novel to support your argument as it relates to the question.

1. _____
_____
_____
_____
_____
_____
_____page:

2. _____
_____
_____
_____
_____
_____
_____page:

List examples SUPPORTING your argument:
_____
_____
_____
_____
_____
_____
_____
_____
_____
_____
_____
_____
_____
_____
_____
_____pages:

List examples COUNTERING your argument:
_____
_____
_____
_____
_____
_____
_____
_____
_____
_____
_____
_____
_____
_____
_____
_____pages:

Name: _____ Date: _____

Socratic Seminar Template – Higher Order: <u>Frankenstein</u> by Mary Shelley

Discussion Question:

Which character in the novel has the best moral compass and why?

Site two main ideas or claims from the novel to support your argument as it relates to the question.

1. _____
_____
_____
_____
_____
_____
_____
_____page:

2. _____
_____
_____
_____
_____
_____
_____
_____page:

List examples SUPPORTING your argument:
_____
_____
_____
_____
_____
_____
_____
_____
_____
_____
_____
_____
_____
_____
_____
_____
_____pages:

List examples COUNTERING your argument:
_____
_____
_____
_____
_____
_____
_____
_____
_____
_____
_____
_____
_____
_____
_____
_____
_____pages:

Socratic Seminar: Participant Rubric

Participants Name: _____ Date: _____

	4	3	2	1
Participant offers solid analysis, without prompting, to move the conversation forward.				
Participant, through his or her comments, demonstrates a depth of understanding of the text.				
Participant, through his or her comments, demonstrates a depth of understanding of the question.				
Participant, through his or her comments, demonstrates he or she has actively listened to other participants.				
Participant offers clarification and follow-up that extends the conversation.				
Participant's remarks and comments refer to specific parts of the text.				
Participant is polite and respectful.				

Teacher comments: _____

_____

_____

_____

_____

_____

Student response to teacher comments: _____

_____

_____

_____

_____

_____

Prompt Title: _____

Frankenstein, or The Modern Prometheus

Chapter Higher Order Comprehension and Analysis Activities

Layout and Instructions

Investigative Clarifier:

Instructions: The first pages of the first two sets of comprehension questions are your Investigative Clarifier Templates. They may be copied and used for any of the chapters or sets of chapters.

For this activity, students will silently read the text, in school or at home, and then work through the Clarifier questions together. Questions and answers will be written on the Investigative Clarifier template.

The clarifying questions revolve around the reader's voice, message, purpose, text structure, argument and other features and then individual ideas are discussed in groups or through a Socratic Seminar.

Again, this activity may be used for any chapter. It may be helpful to assign this activity as a lead into Socratic Seminars.

Higher Order Comprehension and Analysis Activities:

The Higher Order Comprehension and Analysis Activities are designed with the higher order thinking and analytical skills necessary for Common Core State Standards and student 21st Century thinking proficiency in mind. The idea behind this type of activity lies in the knowledge that the key to powerful thinking is in powerful questioning and analysis and in order to help students learn and grow and think to their fullest potential – students must be required to analyze and synthesize and think.

There are Teacher Notes Pages before each set of comprehension questions. The answers to the questions can be found within the teaching pages – for the most part. Some questions require opinions and arguments that will be a student's own. The most important parts of this section are: for students to learn to think critically and for students to support their assertions with actual evidence. As long as those two objectives are found within a student's answers – the student should receive credit. Just as with science – literature analysis must be about discovery – and while there are certain aspects within any work that are given – much of the analysis lies in a student's personal experiences.

By providing students with the basics and letting them explore and verify and support their work – teachers help students learn important life skills essential for many things other than literary analysis. Additionally, by giving students the tools to analyze literature and genres and then letting them explore – students have a greater stake in learning, are more actively engaged and are more apt to retain information.

Teacher Note Pages: Teacher Note Pages are provided for teacher review of the content and for instructional development. Answers to all comprehension questions herein can be found within the corresponding Teacher Note Pages.

The novel begins with a series of letters from an explorer named Robert Walton, to his sister, Margaret Saville. Walton is an established English businessman and the captain of a ship adventuring to the North Pole. The captain's first letter to his sister speaks of preparations for his dangerous voyage. In it he states a desire to accomplish "some great purpose", thus foreshadowing events to come.

Robert will prove important to the story and serve as a voice for narration, but his is more than a voice as he, like Victor, is chasing after the "eternal light" of knowledge. Going where no man has gone...discovering something wonderful and meaningful; however, (spoiler so hold off on this part for instruction) Walton eventually serves as a foil to Victor. While he parallels Victor's ambitious pursuits until near the end, Walton does not follow through – whereas Victor does. Walton is not as obsessed as Victor, or perhaps he is just not courageous enough to allow his passions to overcome him.

In the second letter, Walton demonstrates he is a romantic by allowing his idealism and rebellious nature to emerge. He is also interested in nature...as was a major component within the Romantic Movement. He is voyaging to the North Pole and is in awe of the nature that surrounds him. He admits that his "...daydreams are more extended and magnificent." He also states a "love for the marvelous, a belief in the marvelous..." and this love leads him down his current lonely path.

Walton's second and third letters highlight his isolation as he complains about his lack of friends. His shipmates are not his intellectual equals and he feels separate and alone. The theme of isolation is woven throughout the novel and its characters, thus it is imperative to discuss isolation in detail with students. In these letters, Walton's tone is optimistic and he believes his goals are within reach; only loneliness is never far from the surface and foreshadows events to come.

The fourth letter is the most important. In it Walton uses nature, the weather and a sense of urgency to explain how he and his crew find an emaciated man, also alone, and near death. This letter introduces Victor Frankenstein and the story begins in earnest. Walton now has a friend, an equal, on board his ship and on the surface it appears his loneliness and isolation are over. This will serve to parallel the monster's later desire for a mate and the isolation both the monster and Victor feel.

Isolation and the desire for companionship.

Here is where Walton begins framing the story.

Clarifying Question	Response
What do I understand so far?	
How are the characters interacting with the plot?	
What is the main character's conflict in the letters? Is it internal or external?	

What does the author want the reader to take from letters?

Select a passage. How does this passage illustrate the theme of the story?

Predict what will happen next?

Letters 1-4 Critical Thinking Questions

1. **Prediction:** Who is Robert Walton and what do you think his connection will be to the main character?

_____
_____
_____
_____
_____
_____
_____
_____
_____
_____
_____
_____

2. Summarize the content of the second letter and discuss how Walton shows he is a Romantic through the text.

_____
_____
_____
_____
_____
_____
_____
_____
_____
_____
_____
_____
_____

3. Describe the importance of the fourth letter.

_____
_____
_____
_____
_____
_____
_____
_____
_____
_____
_____

4. After reading the letters, what do you feel about the text so far? Include sensory detail.

_____
_____
_____
_____
_____
_____

Chapter 1

Clarifying Question	Response
What do I understand so far?	
How are the characters interacting with the plot?	
What is the main character's conflict in this chapter? Is it internal or external?	

What does the author want the reader to take from this chapter?

Select a passage. How does this passage illustrate the theme of the story?

Predict what will happen next?

Teacher Note Pages: Chapter 1-2

In Chapter 1, Robert Walton's passenger begins to tell his story and we discover Victor Frankenstein. We learn Victor is from a "good family" and is loved and protected. Through Walton, Victor Frankenstein describes how his childhood companion, and later his wife, enters his life.

In the early version of the novel, Elizabeth is Victor's orphaned cousin. In later versions Elizabeth is found in Italy and adopted. In either story, Victor is around four or five when Elizabeth enters his life. What is clear in both versions is Victor's awe of Elizabeth's beauty and he states that Elizabeth is "...more than a sister – (she is) the beautiful and adored companion of all my occupations and my pleasures." This description is more akin to a thing or a possession than a statement about an equal. Victor clearly believes Elizabeth is his to "...protect, love and cherish." Victor consistently uses the word "mine" when he references Elizabeth. He states: "We called each other familiarly by the name of cousin. No work, no expression could body forth the kind of relation in which she stood to me – my more than sister, since till death she was to be mine only."

Victor has a happy childhood that embodies the exact opposite of isolation. He has a best friend in one of the novel's foil, Henry Clerval, and has a close circle of family and friends. When Victor is a teen he becomes fascinated with the natural world – again a major aspect of the Romantic Movement. Victor desires to learn the secrets of heaven and earth. He is enamored with natural philosophy.

Victor's words and actions indicate he believes women are subservient and must be cared for. An example of this is found in the first paragraph of Chapter 2 when Victor claims he is more than capable of intense application and thirst for knowledge while Elizabeth really can only busy herself "...following the aerial creations of poets...". Victor's statements that Elizabeth cares more for the ascetics of things, while he wants to find out how they work, dismisses the intellectual ability of women – even one raised by his own family. Elizabeth is his possession. Elizabeth is innocent and passive and his to protect and own.

It is important to point out to students that Mary Shelley's mother was an early feminist who wrote prolifically about women and their need for education. And while it seems, especially here in this chapter, that Mary abandoned her mother's ideals, when one looks closer at the statement the author is making about women, they find the opposite is true. Instruct students to really think about the comprehension assignment for Chapter 2 and keep it in mind as they discover the female characters of this novel as well as how both Victor and the monster think about, speak about and react to women and the notion of women in general.

Chapter 1: A Chance to Summarize

The story goes that during the summer of 1816, 18-year-old Mary Shelley and poet Percy Shelley traveled to Geneva, Switzerland to visit their friend Lord Byron. Also present was Byron's friend and doctor, John Polidori. The summer was rainy and the group spent much of their time telling German ghost stories. One day Lord Byron posed a challenge to see which of the group could spin the best supernatural yarn. Walton's letter flows into the narrative. The narrative then flows into more voices. This use of multiple narratives adds layers and lends itself to the feeling of a story being told – reflecting back on Shelley's inspiration – the German ghost stories.

Using the format of the letter, and the Romantic, Gothic style, summarize Chapter 1 below:

_____
_____
_____
_____
_____
_____
_____
_____
_____
_____
_____
_____
_____
_____
_____
_____
_____
_____
_____
_____
_____
_____
_____
_____
_____
_____
_____
_____
_____
_____
_____
_____
_____
_____
_____
_____
_____
_____

Clarifying Question	Response
What do I understand so far?	
How are the characters interacting with the plot?	
What is the main character's conflict in this chapter? Is it internal or external?	

What does the author want the reader to take from this chapter?

Select a passage. How does this passage illustrate the theme of the story?

Predict what will happen next?

Name: _____Date: _____

Chapter 2 Critical Thinking Question

Critical Thinking Prompt: Analyze the first paragraph of Chapter 2 and compare it with the included passage from Chapter 6 of Vindication of the Rights of Woman by Mary Wollstonecraft. Write your analysis on the space provided.

Chapter 2: Frankenstein. *We were brought up together; there was not quite a year difference in our ages. I need not say that we were strangers to any species of disunion or dispute. Harmony was the soul of our companionship, and the diversity and contrast that subsisted in our characters drew us nearer together. Elizabeth was of a calmer and more concentrated disposition; but, with all my ardor, I was capable of a more intense application and was more deeply smitten with the thirst for knowledge. She busied herself with following the aerial creations of the poets; and in the majestic and wondrous scenes which surrounded our Swiss home —the sublime shapes of the mountains, the changes of the seasons, tempest and calm, the silence of winter, and the life and turbulence of our Alpine summers—she found ample scope for admiration and delight. While my companion contemplated with a serious and satisfied spirit the magnificent appearances of things, I delighted in investigating their causes. The world was to me a secret which I desired to divine. Curiosity, earnest research to learn the hidden laws of nature, gladness akin to rapture, as they were unfolded to me, are among the earliest sensations I can remember.*

CHAPTER 6. THE EFFECT WHICH AN EARLY ASSOCIATION OF IDEAS HAS UPON THE CHARACTER.
Vindication of the Rights of Woman by Mary Wollstonecraft

Educated in the enervating style recommended by the writers on whom I have been animadverting; and not having a chance, from their subordinate state in society, to recover their lost ground, is it surprising that women every where appear a defect in nature? Is it surprising, when we consider what a determinate effect an early association of ideas has on the character, that they neglect their understandings, and turn all their attention to their persons?

The great advantages which naturally result from storing the mind with knowledge, are obvious from the following considerations. The association of our ideas is either habitual or instantaneous; and the latter mode seems rather to depend on the original temperature of the mind than on the will. When the ideas, and matters of fact, are once taken in, they lie by for use, till some fortuitous circumstance makes the information dart into the mind with illustrative force, that has been received at very different periods of our lives. Like the lightning's flash are many recollections; one idea assimilating and explaining another, with astonishing rapidity. I do not now allude to that quick perception of truth, which is so intuitive that it baffles research, and makes us at a loss to determine whether it is reminiscence or ratiocination, lost sight of in its celerity, that opens the dark cloud. Over those instantaneous associations we have little power; for when the mind is once enlarged by excursive flights, or profound reflection, the raw materials, will, in some degree, arrange themselves. The understanding, it is true, may keep us from going out of drawing when we group our thoughts, or transcribe from the imagination the warm sketches of fancy; but the animal spirits, the individual character give the colouring. Over this subtile electric fluid, how little power do we possess, and over it how little power can reasᴿ obtain! These fine intractable spirits appear to be the essence of genius, and beaming in its eagle eye, produᴿ in the most eminent degree the happy energy of associating thoughts that surprise, delight, and instruct. Tʼ are the glowing minds that concentrate pictures for their fellow-creatures; forcing them to view with intᴿ the objects reflected from the impassioned imagination, which they passed over in nature.

(*Footnote. I have sometimes, when inclined to laugh at materialists, asked whether, as the powerful effects in nature are apparently produced by fluids, the magnetic, etc. the passions mighʼ volatile fluids that embraced humanity, keeping the more refractory elementary parts together- they were simply a liquid fire that pervaded the more sluggish materials giving them life and ʰ

I must be allowed to explain myself. The generality of people cannot see or feel poetically, they want fancy, and therefore fly from solitude in search of sensible objects; but when an author lends them his eyes, they can see as he saw, and be amused by images they could not select, though lying before them.

Education thus only supplies the man of genius with knowledge to give variety and contrast to his associations; but there is an habitual association of ideas, that grows "with our growth," which has a great effect on the moral character of mankind; and by which a turn is given to the mind, that commonly remains throughout life. So ductile is the understanding, and yet so stubborn, that the associations which depend on adventitious circumstances, during the period that the body takes to arrive at maturity, can seldom be disentangled by reason. One idea calls up another, its old associate, and memory, faithful to the first impressions, particularly when the intellectual powers are not employed to cool our sensations, retraces them with mechanical exactness.

This habitual slavery, to first impressions, has a more baneful effect on the female than the male character, because business and other dry employments of the understanding, tend to deaden the feelings and break associations that do violence to reason. But females, who are made women of when they are mere children, and brought back to childhood when they ought to leave the go-cart forever, have not sufficient strength of mind to efface the superinductions of art that have smothered nature.

Every thing that they see or hear serves to fix impressions, call forth emotions, and associate ideas, that give a sexual character to the mind. False notions of beauty and delicacy stop the growth of their limbs and produce a sickly soreness, rather than delicacy of organs; and thus weakened by being employed in unfolding instead of examining the first associations, forced on them by every surrounding object, how can they attain the vigour necessary to enable them to throw off their factitious character?—where find strength to recur to reason and rise superior to a system of oppression, that blasts the fair promises of spring? This cruel association of ideas, which every thing conspires to twist into all their habits of thinking, or, to speak with more precision, of feeling, receives new force when they begin to act a little for themselves; for they then perceive, that it is only through their address to excite emotions in men, that pleasure and power are to be obtained. Besides, all the books professedly written for their instruction, which make the first impression on their minds, all inculcate the same opinions. Educated in worse than Egyptian bondage, it is unreasonable, as well as cruel, to upbraid them with faults that can scarcely be avoided, unless a degree of native vigour be supposed, that falls to the lot of very few amongst mankind.

For instance, the severest sarcasms have been levelled against the sex, and they have been ridiculed for repeating "a set of phrases learnt by rote," when nothing could be more natural, considering the education they receive, and that their "highest praise is to obey, unargued"—the will of man. If they are not allowed to have reason sufficient to govern their own conduct—why, all they learn—must be learned by rote! And when all their ingenuity is called forth to adjust their dress, "a passion for a scarlet coat," is so natural, that it never surprised me; and, allowing Pope's summary of their character to be just, "that every woman is at heart a rake," why should they be bitterly censured for seeking a congenial mind, and preferring a rake to a man of sense?

Rakes know how to work on their sensibility, whilst the modest merit of reasonable men has, of course, less effect on their feelings, and they cannot reach the heart by the way of the understanding, because they have few sentiments in common.

It seems a little absurd to expect women to be more reasonable than men in their LIKINGS, and still to deny them the uncontroled use of reason. When do men FALL IN LOVE with sense? When do they, with their superior powers and advantages, turn from the person to the mind? And how can they then expect women, who are only taught to observe behaviour, and acquire manners rather than morals, to despise what they have been all their lives labouring to attain? Where are they suddenly to find judgment enough to weigh patiently the sense of an awkward virtuous man, when his manners, of which they are made critical judges, are rebuffing, and his conversation cold and dull, because it does not consist of pretty repartees, or well-turned compliments? In order to admire or esteem any thing for a continuance, we must, at least, have our curiosity excited by knowing, in some degree, what we admire; for we are unable to estimate the value of qualities and virtues above our omprehension. Such a respect, when it is felt, may be very sublime; and the confused consciousness of humility may render the dependent creature an interesting object, in some points of view; but human love must have grosser ingredients; and the person very naturally will come in for its share—and, an ample share it mostly has!

Love is, in a great degree, an arbitrary passion, and will reign like some other stalking mischiefs, by its own authority, without deigning to reason; and it may also be easily distinguished from esteem, the foundation of friendship, because it is often excited by evanescent beauties and graces, though to give an energy to the sentiment something more solid must deepen their impression and set the imagination to work, to make the most fair— the first good.

Common passions are excited by common qualities. Men look for beauty and the simper of good humoured docility: women are captivated by easy manners: a gentleman-like man seldom fails to please them, and their thirsty ears eagerly drink the insinuating nothings of politeness, whilst they turn from the unintelligible sounds of the charmer—reason, charm he never so wisely. With respect to superficial accomplishments, the rake certainly has the advantage; and of these, females can form an opinion, for it is their own ground. Rendered gay and giddy by the whole tenor of their lives, the very aspect of wisdom, or the severe graces of virtue must have a lugubrious appearance to them; and produce a kind of restraint from which they and love, sportive child, naturally revolt. Without taste, excepting of the lighter kind, for taste is the offspring of judgment, how can they discover, that true beauty and grace must arise from the play of the mind? and how can they be expected to relish in a lover what they do not, or very imperfectly, possess themselves? The sympathy that unites hearts, and invites to confidence, in them is so very faint, that it cannot take fire, and thus mount to passion. No, I repeat it, the love cherished by such minds, must have grosser fuel!

The inference is obvious; till women are led to exercise their understandings, they should not be satirized for their attachment to rakes; nor even for being rakes at heart, when it appears to be the inevitable consequence of their education. They who live to please must find their enjoyments, their happiness, in pleasure! It is a trite, yet true remark, that we never do any thing well, unless we love it for its own sake.

Supposing, however, for a moment, that women were, in some future revolution of time, to become, what I sincerely wish them to be, even love would acquire more serious dignity, and be purified in its own fires; and virtue giving true delicacy to their affections, they would turn with disgust from a rake. Reasoning then, as well as feeling, the only province of woman, at present, they might easily guard against exterior graces, and quickly learn to despise the sensibility that had been excited and hackneyed in the ways of women, whose trade was vice; and allurement's wanton airs. They would recollect that the flame, (one must use appropriate expressions,) which they wished to light up, had been exhausted by lust, and that the sated appetite, losing all relish for pure and simple pleasures, could only be roused by licentious arts of variety. What satisfaction could a woman of delicacy promise herself in a union with such a man, when the very artlessness of her affection might appear insipid? Thus does Dryden describe the situation:

"Where love is duty on the female side,
On theirs mere sensual gust, and sought with surly pride."

But one grand truth women have yet to learn, though much it imports them to act accordingly. In the choice of a husband they should not be led astray by the qualities of a lover—for a lover the husband, even supposing him to be wise and virtuous, cannot long remain.

Were women more rationally educated, could they take a more comprehensive view of things, they would be contented to love but once in their lives; and after marriage calmly let passion subside into friendship—into that tender intimacy, which is the best refuge from care; yet is built on such pure, still affections, that idle jealousies would not be allowed to disturb the discharge of the sober duties of life, nor to engross the thoughts that ought to be otherwise employed. This is a state in which many men live; but few, very few women. And the difference may easily be accounted for, without recurring to a sexual character. Men, for whom we are told women are made, have too much occupied the thoughts of women; and this association has so entangled love, with all their motives of action; and, to harp a little on an old string, having been solely employed either to prepare themselves to excite love, or actually putting their lessons in practice, they cannot live without love. But, when a sense of duty, or fear of shame, obliges them to restrain this pampered desire of pleasing beyond certain lengths, too far for delicacy, it is true, though far from criminality, they obstinately determine to love, I speak of their passion, their husbands to the end of the chapter—and then acting the part which they foolishly exacted from their lovers, they become abject wooers, and fond slaves.

Men of wit and fancy are often rakes; and fancy is the food of love. Such men will inspire passion. Half the sex, in its present infantine state, would pine for a Lovelace; a man so witty, so graceful, and so valiant; and can they DESERVE blame for acting according to principles so constantly inculcated? They want a lover and protector: and behold him kneeling before them—bravery prostrate to beauty! The virtues of a husband are thus thrown by love into the background, and gay hopes, or lively emotions, banish reflection till the day of reckoning comes; and come it surely will, to turn the sprightly lover into a surly suspicious tyrant, who contemptuously insults the very weakness he fostered. Or, supposing the rake reformed, he cannot quickly get rid of old habits. When a man of abilities is first carried away by his passions, it is necessary that sentiment and taste varnish the enormities of vice, and give a zest to brutal indulgences: but when the gloss of novelty is worn off, and pleasure palls upon the sense, lasciviousness becomes barefaced, and enjoyment only the desperate effort of weakness flying from reflection as from a legion of devils. Oh! virtue, thou art not an empty name! All that life can give— thou givest!

If much comfort cannot be expected from the friendship of a reformed rake of superior abilities, what is the consequence when he lacketh sense, as well as principles? Verily misery in its most hideous shape. When the habits of weak people are consolidated by time, a reformation is barely possible; and actually makes the beings miserable who have not sufficient mind to be amused by innocent pleasure; like the tradesman who retires from the hurry of business, nature presents to them only a universal blank; and the restless thoughts prey on the damped spirits. Their reformation as well as his retirement actually makes them wretched, because it deprives them of all employment, by quenching the hopes and fears that set in motion their sluggish minds.

If such be the force of habit; if such be the bondage of folly, how carefully ought we to guard the mind from storing up vicious associations; and equally careful should we be to cultivate the understanding, to save the poor wight from the weak dependent state of even harmless ignorance. For it is the right use of reason alone which makes us independent of every thing—excepting the unclouded Reason—"Whose service is perfect freedom."

_____
_____
_____
_____
_____
_____
_____
_____
_____
_____
_____
_____
_____
_____
_____
_____
_____
_____
_____
_____
_____
_____
_____

Teacher Note Pages: Chapters 3-5

The conflict between science and nature come alive in this section of <u>Frankenstein</u>. In Chapter 3, Victor goes off to college in Ingolstadt. He attends a chemistry lecture by a Professor Waldman and is convinced to pursue his studies in science.

Chapter 4 begins Victor's obsessive pursuit of scientific knowledge and subsequently the creation of life. He works tirelessly, studying anatomy and death and everything his professors have to teach. He contemplates life and zealously considers the notion of being able to bring life back to that which is dying. This is a constant medical pursuit and not without ethical consideration and religious implication, not the least of which is the god-like act of creation. This is an interesting topic to students – and one that is still controversial today.

Discuss With Students:

> *"No one can conceive the variety of feelings which bore me onwards, like a hurricane, in the first enthusiasm of success. Life and death appeared to me ideal bounds, which I should first break through, and pour a torrent of light into our dark world. A new species would bless me as its creator and source; many happy and excellent natures would owe their being to me. No father could claim the gratitude of his child so completely as I should deserve theirs. Pursuing these reflections, I thought that if I could bestow animation upon lifeless matter, I might in process of time (although I now found it impossible) renew life where death had apparently devoted the body to corruption.*

As Chapter 4 closes so does a cycle of seasons and the reader sees Victor transforming. As his quest for the creation of life progresses, Victor undergoes a metamorphosis, transforming from the embodiment of a human being to a soul who is nervous, incapable of relaxation, pale, and hallow…as if in creating life…he himself is dying.

In Chapter 5 Victor's dream is realized and the monster becomes animated; only when Victor sees his creation he is horrified. He leaves the monster, but when he tries to sleep he is troubled by nightmares. When he wakes, the monster is hovering over his bed.

Discuss With Students:

> *"…when, by the dim and yellow light of the moon, as it forced its way through the window shutters, I beheld the wretch—the miserable monster whom I had created. He held up the curtain of the bed; and his eyes, if eyes they may be called, were fixed on me. His jaws opened, and he muttered some inarticulate sounds, while a grin wrinkled his cheeks. He might have spoken, but I did not hear; one hand was stretched out, seemingly to detain me, but I escaped and rushed downstairs. I took refuge in the courtyard belonging to the house which I inhabited, where I remained during the rest of the night, walking up and down in the greatest agitation, listening attentively, catching and fearing each sound as if it were to announce the approach of the demoniacal corpse to which I had so miserably given life.*

Victor goes to town and meets an old friend, Henry Clerval, who has come to attend the university. Clerval is a close intimate friend of not only Victor, but of Victor's family.

Victor takes his friend, Henry, home with him. The monster is gone. Victor grows terribly ill and Henry must nurse him back to health. In an ironic turn of events, Victor has created life and is now deathly ill. As the Chapter closes Henry has skipped a season of studies to help Victor to health. With Victor recovering, Henry presents him with a letter from Elizabeth.

In Chapters 3-5 the impending doom of the earlier chapters has been realized and Victor's pursuit of a noble and awesome scientific discovery have crippled into the creation of a grotesque being. The nightmares that haunt

Victor the first night of the monster's animation foreshadow impending tragedy.

The images conjured of Elizabeth foretell of a grave future:

> *But it was in vain; I slept, indeed, but I was disturbed by the wildest dreams. I thought I saw Elizabeth, in the bloom of health, walking in the streets of Ingolstadt. Delighted and surprised, I embraced her, but as I imprinted the first kiss on her lips, they became livid with the hue of death; her features appeared to change, and I thought that I held the corpse of my dead mother in my arms; a shroud enveloped her form, and I saw the grave-worms crawling in the folds of the flannel. I started from my sleep with horror; a cold dew covered my forehead, my teeth chattered, and every limb became convulsed; when, by the dim and yellow light of the moon, as it forced its way through the window shutters, I beheld the wretch—the miserable monster whom I had created.*

Discuss: Victor views science as the only way to gain true knowledge, but what of the knowledge when it manifests into a monster? What of the heavily guarded secrets of science and the discoveries thereof?

Shelley uses the symbolism of light and darkness. In Walton's earlier letter (the first) there is mention of eternal light – now when Victor describes uncovering the secret of life he claims that the discovery comes out of the "darkness"… and that "a sudden light broke" upon him. Light reveals and it can blind.

In these Chapters, Victor addresses Walton – reminding the reader of the multiple layers of storytelling occurring within the text – perhaps stemming from the German ghost stories Mary Shelley and her friends at Lake Geneva told during the summer in which the monster was conceived. Shelley uses a narrative frame to tell Victor's tale. A narrative frame is a complex layering technique to introduce a story using another story. The frame establishes a way to shift perspective. The primary narrator is Captain Robert Walton – a man on a scientific adventure to the Arctic. In letters to his sister, Walton begins retelling the story being told to him by a man found stranded on the ice, "the stranger". The theme of the important place secrecy holds, in relation to science, is protected in that Victor told his story to another scientist – who is in turn also passing it along.

The theme of secrecy and the shroud thereof unveils itself in Chapters 3-5. Victor withdraws from his friends, his loves and his family and turns within – and the more he discovers, the more withdrawn and secretive he becomes – actually losing some of his humanity and rendering himself ghastly ill. Victor is happy to see Henry, but Henry's presence makes Victor full of regret and remorse for what he has done/created.   Real humanity replaces the hideous scientifically created monster in the embodiment of Henry. Victor is happy to see his friend; however, he guards his secret cautiously.

It is interesting to explain to students that some people believe Mary's future husband, Percy Bysshe Shelley, who was with her at Lake Geneva when she wrote <u>Frankenstein,</u> was fond of using the apostrophe as a literary device and ask them to draw comparisons between the works of both authors – if time permits. Students find the back-story interesting – it makes literature come alive.

Name: _____ Date: _____

Chapters 3-5 Critical Thinking Question

1. How can science and the quest for knowledge lead to ethical conflicts? _____

_____

_____

_____

_____

_____

_____

_____

_____

_____

_____

_____

_____

2. Discuss the irony of Victor's failing health and seemingly loss of humanity as the monster comes to life. _____

_____

_____

_____

_____

_____

_____

_____

_____

_____

_____

_____

_____

3. Predict the fate of Elizabeth in a narrative with a beginning, a middle and an end. _____

_____

_____

_____

_____

_____

_____

_____

_____

_____

_____

_____

_____

_____

_____

_____

_____

Clarifying Question	Response
What do I understand so far?	
How are the characters interacting with the plot?	
What is the main character's conflict in this chapter? Is it internal or external?	

What does the author want the reader to take from this chapter?

Select a passage. How does this passage illustrate the theme of the story

Predict what will happen next?

Teacher Note Pages: Chapters 6-8

Chapter 6: Elizabeth's letter to Victor expresses her concern for his health and her desire for him to write home in his own hand – even just one word. She also tells him about Justine, who is a favorite of Victor's. Justine is a neighbor and is one of many children, the least favorite of her own parents and abused by her mother. The Frankenstein's take her in and are kind to her. When Elizabeth's aunt dies, the girl stays with the family, only one by one Justine's own siblings die and she must move home to care for her ailing mother – who is alternately remorseful for the way she's treated Justine and then blaming Justine for the death of her other children. Justine's mother dies and Justine returns to the Frankenstein's and is reported to be happy and pretty. Little William is also reported to be a happy and adorable young boy. William is Victor's younger brother and the darling of the family.

Victor writes Elizabeth back – which tires him dreadfully. When he recovers he shows his friend Henry around the university. Henry is there to study the East and Victor decides to stay and join him – while Clerval studies the languages – Victor studies the humanities. Victor's plans to go home are delayed by his new studies. Victor and Henry take an adventure through nature – leaving one to wonder what will happen. The presence of "nature providing an emotional experience" was part of the Romantic Movement. The evidence of nature on mood is present throughout the novel – here bringing Victor from his depression – if only temporarily.

Henry provides a bridge between the dark depths and isolation Victor has fallen into back to his family and society. Henry is Victor's foil – open, honest, happy and clear.

Chapter 7: When Victor and Henry return, something dreadful has indeed happened. Victor's father writes that poor little William is dead. Victor leaves for Geneva immediately. By the time he arrives home the gates to Geneva are closed and he spends the evening walking in the woods. He walks to where his poor little brother William was killed and sees the monster. He knows in his heart that the monster is responsible for the child's death. The next morning he returns home and discovers that Justine has been accused of the murder because they find a picture of Caroline Frankenstein on her person – a picture they believe William had last – only the monster carefully planted it on the girl.

Victor is afraid to really stand up for Justine for fear he will be labeled insane.

Chapter 8: Chapter 8 opens with the darkness of Victor's remorse and guilt:

> *"During the whole of this wretched mockery of justice I suffered living torture. It was to be decided, whether the result of my curiosity and lawless devices would cause the death of two of my fellow-beings: one a smiling babe, full of innocence and joy; the other far more dreadfully murdered, with every aggravation of infamy that could make the murder memorable in horror. Justine also was a girl of merit, and possessed qualities which promised to render her life happy: now all was to be obliterated in an ignominious grave; and I the cause! A thousand times rather would I have confessed myself guilty of the crime ascribed to Justine; but I was absent when it was committed, and such a declaration would have been considered as the ravings of a madman, and would not have exculpated her who suffered through me."*

Justine confesses to a crime she did not commit and when questioned by Elizabeth as to why she replied that hell and damnation were threatened – she states she began to feel that she was the monster they were telling her she was.

The chapter ends with Victor foreshadowing more doom as he states that William and Justine were the *"first hapless victims of his unhallowed arts."*

The theme of the passive role of women is present in these chapters. Elizabeth stands up for Justine; however, she is powerless to help her. Victor, the man, is the only one with the power to help the proverbial damsel in distress but he does not.

As you discuss how the female characters unfold, ask students to review their comprehension question answers from Chapter 2, share them with their neighbors and compare them to the theme of the passive role of women in this chapter.

Teacher Notes:

Name: _____Date: _____

Chapters 6-8 Critical Thinking Questions

1. By incorporating written letters into the story, Elizabeth and Alphonse are allowed to participate in the narrative and make Victor seem more human and alive. Do you agree or disagree. Please support your answer with details from the novel. _____
_____
_____
_____
_____
_____
_____
_____
_____
_____
_____
_____
_____

2. What role are women playing in the narrative? _____
_____
_____
_____
_____
_____
_____
_____
_____
_____
_____
_____
_____

3. Henry serves as a road back to his family for Victor. Describe the progress of Victor's isolation and subsequent return. _____
_____
_____
_____
_____
_____
_____
_____
_____
_____
_____
_____

4. Site an example of foreshadowing in Chapters 6-8 and predict what may happen. _____

_____

_____

_____

_____

_____

_____

_____

_____

_____

_____

5. Why is Victor consumed with guilt over Justine's conviction? _____

_____

_____

_____

_____

_____

_____

_____

_____

_____

_____

6. In Chapter 7, what does Victor discover when he is locked out of the gates of Geneva? _____

_____

_____

_____

_____

_____

_____

_____

_____

7. Describe your favorite passage of the novel Frankenstein so far. _____

_____

_____

_____

_____

_____

_____

_____

Active Reading: Character Traits and Motives

Instructions: In the space below, please describe Victor, his character traits and his character motives.

Character Trait: When we talk about a character, we often describe that character in terms of *character traits*. A character trait is a descriptive adjective like *happy or sad* that tells the specific qualities of a character.

Character traits are the kind of words we use to describe ourselves or others. Here you are using the same kind of words to describe fictional characters!

Character Motive: *Character motives* are the reasons behind what characters do. They are the reason for character actions. ***They are the reasons why***.

Think in terms of what motivates you. Do you get good grades? Why? What motivates you? Is it to do your best? Is it to play sports? What is your motivation?

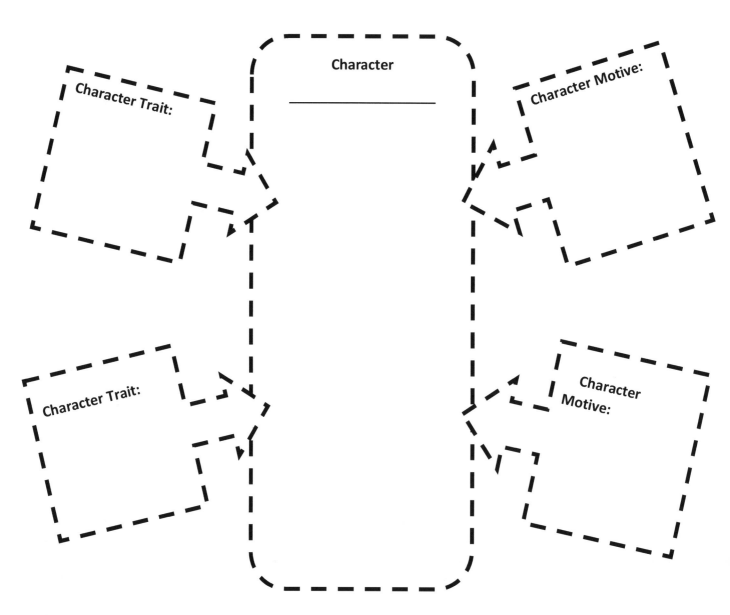

Character

_____

Character Trait:

Character Trait:

Character Motive:

Character Motive:

Name: _____Date: _____

Chapters 6-8 Character Traits Revealed

Authors reveal character traits directly, using descriptions, or indirectly, in what characters say and do, in how they act and feel and behave. Please interpret the following passages in relation to what the words reveal about Victor. Be sure to indicate if the characterization is direct or indirect.

1. In her Chapter 6 letter: Elizabeth writes: "You will find a happy, cheerful home and friends who love you dearly". _____
_____
_____
_____
_____ **Direct or Indirect**

2. Victor exclaims upon reading Elizabeth's letter: "Dear, dear Elizabeth!" I exclaimed, when I had read her letter: "I will write instantly and relieve them from the anxiety they must feel".
_____
_____
_____
_____ **Direct or Indirect**

3. Victor's narrative: "Summer passed away in these occupations, and my return to Geneva was … delayed by several accidents, winter and snow arrived, the roads were deemed impassable, and my journey was retarded until the ensuing spring. I felt this delay very bitterly; for I longed to see my native town and my beloved friends. My return had only been delayed so long, from an unwillingness to leave Clerval in a strange place, before he had become acquainted with any of its inhabitants."
_____
_____
_____
_____ **Direct or Indirect**

4. Victor's narrative: We passed a few sad hours until eleven o'clock, when the trial was to commence. My father and the rest of the family being obliged to attend as witnesses, I accompanied them to the court. During the whole of this wretched mockery of justice I suffered living torture. It was to be decided whether the result of my curiosity and lawless devices would cause the death of two of my fellow beings….Justine also was a girl of merit and possessed qualities which promised to render her life happy; now all was to be obliterated in an ignominious grave, and I the cause! A thousand times rather would I have confessed myself guilty of the crime ascribed to Justine, but I was absent when it was committed, and such a declaration would have been considered as the ravings of a madman and would not have exculpated her who suffered through me.
_____
_____
_____
_____ **Direct or Indirect**

Teacher Note Pages: Chapters 9-10

Chapter 9: Victor sinks into depression with thoughts of Justine's execution at his own inadvertent hands. He considers taking his own life but there are Elizabeth and his father to consider. His father is worried about him so the entire family travels to their home in Belrive. Victor is happier there. In Geneva, the gates of the town close at 10 o'clock and Victor feels trapped, but in Belrive Victor is free to wander the countryside and row onto the lake at all hours when sleep escapes him. While the trip is helpful it does not cure Victor's mood or conscience. In this chapter, and the next, nature and its influence have noticeable effects on Victor and his moods – again very symbolic in Romantic Movement and Gothic literature.

Chapter 10: To cheer himself up, Victor decides to hike to the summit of Montanvert . Unfortunately, as he is out, he encounters the monster. The monster begs Victor to be his ally and to assume the role necessitated by being the creature's creator. The monster is eloquent telling Victor he will be all that is good should Victor not shun him. Victor curses the monster, but in the end Victor is persuaded to listen to his story. The power of nature to help Victor out of his depression, if only momentarily, is symbolic and omnipotent and serves to remind the reader that Victor is only human. Victor comments on how nature can sooth his pain, but nature can also cause destruction. As Victor is high in the mountaintops, a storm brews below, foreshadowing a foreboding event to come. Point out to students that Shelley uses weather as a signal throughout the novel. Remind students...or get them to remind you, that when Victor tempted nature, by creating a being, the results were not good.

In Chapter 10, while it is Victor cursing the monster – it is the monster that is eloquent and human-like – thus narrowing the gap between human and beast. The monster compares Victor to God and lays the responsibility of the monster's evil doings on his creator – stating that he is Victor's creation and should be his Adam rather than his fallen angel.

Ask students to discuss the following questions in groups or pairs and instruct them to be prepared to share their answers with the group. **Questions:**

1. *How does Victor compare to the monster at this stage of the story?*
2. *How does nature affect Victor in these chapters?*
3. *How do you feel about Victor shunning the monster?*
4. *How is the gap between human and monster closing? Provide specific evidence.*

Teacher Notes:

Chapters 9-10 Critical Thinking Questions

1. What specifically helps Victor realize he has created more than a scientific product? Elaborate. _____

_____

_____

_____

_____

_____

_____

_____

_____

_____

2. Articulate the main idea of Chapter 10. _____

_____

_____

_____

_____

_____

_____

_____

_____

_____

3. Describe the evidence of the Gothic-novel present in Chapters 9 and 10. _____

_____

_____

_____

_____

_____

_____

_____

4. Does the monster blame Victor for the monster's own actions? Why or why not? _____

_____

_____

_____

_____

_____

_____

_____

_____

Activity Instructions: Making Inferences Partner Talk

Ask students to consider Chapter 10 and what it foreshadows. Have students fill out the activity sheet titled, **Making Inferences Partner Talk.** After their worksheets are complete, pair up students and ask them to discuss their answers and be prepared to share their results. Ask students to agree on one instance of foreshadowing per pair or group to discuss.

After students discuss in pairs, call for predictions from each group. Note the predictions and mark the ones off that come true later in the book.

At the end of the entire unit – have students discuss which instances of foreshadowing came to fruition and which did not.

Examples of Foreshadowing in Chapter 10:

Foreshadow Example 1: Arriving at the top of the ascent, Victor looks down over the river to see the "vast mists" arising. His ascent to the top foreshadows that only the climb down is left – or the fall that is to come: that of Victor into yet more moral transgressions, and the fall of the monster into a more hideous being as a result of Victor's treatment of him.

Foreshadow Example 2: In Chapter 10, Victor dreams of a very large group of beings surrounding him – foreshadowing the reappearance of the monster.

Foreshadow Example 3: In the last paragraph of Chapter 10, the rain begins to fall as Frankenstein and the monster enter the monster's hut. Rain symbolizes a cleansing – yet the cleansing rain begins as the monster and Frankenstein enter a hut, shielding themselves from the purifying effects of the water. Additionally there is a fire inside of the hut. Fire is demonic and villainous – often symbolizing destruction – foretelling the destruction to come.

Foreshadow Example 4: In both Chapters 9 and 10, Victor is surrounded by ice, which represents ignorance and darkness. He does not understand the monster nor does he understand the consequences of his actions towards the monster – just as he did not understand the consequence of creating the monster. Light, in the form of fire, in contrast, enters the chapter only after the monster appears and takes Victor to his hut to tell his tale.

Activity Making Inferences Partner Talk

Your Turn: Select two events and make inferences about what will happen later in the story.

Character or Event:	
Details from the Story:	**Foreshadowing Prediction:**
Come back and analyze:	

Character or Event:	
Details from the Story:	**Foreshadowing Prediction:**
Come back and analyze:	

Teacher Note Pages Chapters 11 and 12

Chapter 11: The monster tells Victor of his confusion and how he assimilated into the human world. He confesses to confusing early events but he remembers when he first realized sensations...hearing, feeling, smelling...being. The monster describes light as oppressive and darkness, while desolate, comforting. Eventually the monster tells of finding fire and discovering its usefulness for cooking.

The monster stumbles upon the very hut they are in. The old man who occupies it flees in terror. The monster ventures to the village – where people flee at the sight of him as well. Hurt and further isolated, the monster decides to stay away from humans and live in isolation.

One night the monster takes refuge in a small room next to a cottage. He watches the occupants of the cottage living a happy normal life and seems to pine for the same. He is intrigued by their happenings and enchanted with the music they play, the life they live and little things, such as how they use taper candles to prolong the light and, inadvertently, the pleasure of his viewing. He is enthralled at their humanness.

Chapter 12: The monster watches the neighbors and notices that they do not always seem happy. He realizes this is because they are poor. He feels remorse for stealing their food to sustain his life. He grows deeply affected by their sadness. The monster displays human traits when he is emotionally moved by the fact that the young couple often goes hungry because they feed the blind old man before eating anything themselves.

The monster also notices the young man spends much of his time cutting wood to keep his family warm, so at night the monster takes his tools and cuts wood for him. The monster is developing human compassion and feeling and while we understand he committed the horrendous murder of William and caused the death of Justine – we can sympathize with him. Over the course of this chapter, the monster grows and seems to be developing into a better being than he was before.

The monster notices, because he is now chopping wood for the family, the young man is able to stay home and all seem happier. The monster seems pleased that his deed allowed the young man to stay home and make repairs to the cottage. It was by watching this family, through an entire winter, that the monster learned to speak. He notices that the people he observes are an old man and his young adult children and that even through their poverty they were kind. He admires their lovely physical forms and grows to despise his grotesque one.

The monster suffers in isolation at the kindness and love of the family. The fonder he grows of them the more isolated he feels. The family's warm interactions serve to pain the monster as he lacks the companionship he now longs for. The more he knows, the more he learns, the more isolated he feels. Knowledge is coming at a price. The monster, not unlike Victor, becomes aware of nature's power and begins to recognize the danger possessing knowledge can bring.

As the novel progresses and the monster continues to tell his story, the reader discovers that the monster and Frankenstein are more alike than they are different. This is augmented by the narration and its melodramatic tone. The monster speaks through the story told by Victor, whose story is being told by Watson – who is ultimately speaking in the romantic tone of Shelley.

Name: _____ Date: _____

Chapters 11-12 Critical Thinking Questions

1. Re-read the first three paragraphs of Chapter 11 and elaborate on your thoughts and *feelings* regarding the difficult awakening of the monster as he truly comes to life. _____

_____

_____

_____

_____

_____

_____

_____

_____

_____

2. Discuss how the feeling of the family's warm interactions affects the monster. _____

_____

_____

_____

_____

_____

_____

_____

_____

_____

_____

_____

3. How does the tone of the narrative help the monster and Victor as they align into almost a parallel being? _____

_____

_____

_____

_____

_____

4. Who seems the better human in Chapter 12, Victor or the monster? Support your answer. _____

_____

_____

_____

_____

_____

Teacher Note Pages: Chapters 13 and 14

Chapter 13 and 14: The monster learns the young man's name is Felix, the young woman, Felix's sister, is named Agatha and the old blind man is De Lacey, their father.

One day a visitor arrives at the cottage. She is a young woman who speaks a different language, but is welcomed and brightens the mood of the humans who live there. The monster notices a stress seems to be lifted from the cottage residents. He also notices that the stranger is accepted even though she is different. This fact causes him to wonder if the visitor speaking a different language, yet still being welcomed, should cause him to be hopeful for his own acceptance. She is different, the monster reasons, but she is accepted and welcomed, so perhaps there is hope for him after all.

The monster notes that Felix calls her *"his little Arabian"* and is overjoyed to see this beautiful woman – who does not understand his words but is thrilled to see him anyway – thrilled and something else as the monster notices her tears. He is noticing emotion – humanness. The monster now realizes the days pass as they previously had, but where there was once sadness at the cottage – happiness now reigns.

As the young man, Felix, teaches the girl their native language, the monster learns to speak as well – he is bridging a difference between him and the cottagers as is the stranger – whose name is Safie. Learning to speak, and therefore communicate, further humanizes the monster.

Again, the monster learns many things as Felix teaches the young lady*: "The book from which Felix instructed Safie was Volney's Ruins of Empires. I should not have understood the purport of this book had not Felix, in reading it, given very minute explanations. He had chosen this work, he said, because the declamatory style was framed in imitation of the Eastern authors. Through this work I obtained a cursory knowledge of history and a view of the several empires at present existing in the world; it gave me an insight into the manners, governments, and religions of the different nations of the earth. I heard of the slothful Asiatics, of the stupendous genius and mental activity of the Grecians, of the wars and wonderful virtue of the early Romans—of their subsequent degenerating—of the decline of that mighty empire, of chivalry, Christianity, and kings. I heard of the discovery of the American hemisphere and wept with Safie over the hapless fate of its original inhabitants."*

The parallel education the monster is receiving changes him. *"Every conversation of the cottagers now opened new wonders to me. While I listened to the instructions which Felix bestowed upon the Arabian, the strange system of human society was explained to me. I heard of the division of property, of immense wealth and squalid poverty, of rank, descent, and noble blood."* He began to understand that people and creatures have a place and this leads him to understand his place and his rank...or lack thereof.

The theme of knowledge is power rears and is put forth as evil in the monster's words and realizations: *"Of what a strange nature is knowledge! It clings to the mind when it has once seized on it like a lichen on the rock. I wished sometimes to shake off all thought and feeling, but I learned that there was but one means to overcome the sensation of pain, and that was death—a state which I feared yet did not understand. I admired virtue and good feelings and loved the gentle manners and amiable qualities of my cottagers, but I was shut out from intercourse with them, except through means which I obtained by stealth, when I was unseen and unknown, and which rather increased than satisfied the desire I had of becoming one among my fellows. The gentle words of Agatha and the animated smiles of the charming Arabian were not for me. The mild exhortations of the old man and the lively conversation of the loved Felix were not for me. Miserable, unhappy wretch!*

The monster discovers the family, Felix, Agatha and their father De Lacey, were exiled from France and stripped of their wealth. It is important to discuss why Mary Shelley put Safie into the novel as she is not the stereotypical female character within this novel. What about the theme? And Shelley's views of the female archetype?

The monster learns that this once wealthy family he has been living through, was put to ruins as the result of Safie's father – a Turkish, civil servant unjustly treated. When Felix tired to help Safie's father out of the injustice, the man promised Felix Safie as a wife; when the promise was delivered upon, Safie's father changed his mind; because, he did not want his daughter to marry a Christian. Then, because the family helped the Turkish man escape from France, Felix, Agatha and De Lacey were exiled. Once back in Constantinople with her father – Safie escaped and reunited with Felix.

Days passed, the monster notes and then proudly boasts to his creator that he learned to both speak and read more rapidly than Safie. The more he understood, the monster explains, the more he heard and the deeper his knowledge grew of life and wealth and property and poverty. This knowledge brought him to realize that his creator left him with no money or power or property or beauty. He discovers that he is a hideous being – deformed and loathsome. This knowledge brings him agony. He tried to suppress the pain as he watched the family, but could not. He also learned that the father, DeLacey, treats the girls differently than he treats the boy and that his creator did not bless him with a mother or a female partner. The monster again feels isolated and alone – more knowledge – more isolation.

The monster's intrigue of the relationship between Felix and Safie lies in his desire for Victor to accept him. Felix's willingness to risk everything for the sake of someone who has been unjustly punished, gives the monster hope that Victor will recognize the hurtful injustice of abandoning him. The monster was abandoned by his creator for his outward appearance and he finds hope in the relationships of the cottagers that he can change that. They, after all, risked and lost everything they had for another – so cannot his creator accept the one he has brought to life? However, just as Felix's bravery, in helping Safie's father escape, stands in stark contrast to Victor's shameful unwillingness to save Justine, so does Felix's compassion for Safie underscore Victor's bitter hatred for the monster. Victor will not accept him.

These chapters once again highlight the idea of submissive and subservient woman who submit to the power of men. Justine is one, Elizabeth is one and even Agatha is one; Safie, however is not. Safie boldly counters this stereotype by rejecting her father's attempt to return her to a life of limitations in Constantinople. By striking out on her own, even in the face of uncertainty, Safie instantly becomes a character of strength and fortitude in the novel. The fact that Safie's role is minor actually adds emphasis to the rarity of her actions and strength within the Gothic genre. Like her father and the monster, Safie is an outsider -- only she – the woman – manages to gain acceptance – where the monster cannot.

Chapters 13-14 Critical Thinking Questions

1. Think about Chapter 14. How are the monster and Safie alike? How are they different? _____

_____
_____
_____
_____
_____
_____
_____
_____

2. The monster says: *"Of what a strange nature is knowledge! It clings to the mind when it has once seized on it like a lichen on the rock."* Elaborate from his point of view. _____

_____
_____
_____
_____
_____
_____
_____

3. Think about the content of Chapters 13 and 14 and how outsiders are treated. Relate this to the way outsiders are treated today. Remember to site specific examples from the text. _____

_____
_____
_____
_____
_____
_____
_____
_____
_____
_____
_____
_____
_____
_____

Teacher Note Pages: Chapters 15-17

Chapter 15: Through the cottagers, the monster comes to find value in the virtues they possess. But the more human the monster becomes, the more he longs to interact. One day while looking for food in the woods, the monster finds a bag containing books and clothes. One of the books is Paradise Lost and since he doesn't understand what fiction is – reads it as history and draws a parallel between it and his own life.

The monster realizes that he has journal notes in his own pocket – pockets of the clothes he took when he left Victor. He can now read and discovers that his own creator was horrified and disgusted by him. The monster longs to be accepted more than ever and hopes the cottagers can see past his exterior to the "human" inside – the human they helped to form – not literally but in very real terms.

De Lacey is blind, so the monster decides to approach him first. De Lacey would be the least prejudiced by the monster's form because he couldn't see it. One day, when the other three are out for a walk, the monster enters the cottage and speaks to the old man. All is spoiled when the others return, are horrified by the monster's appearance and proceed to drive him away.

Chapter 16: The monster sadly flees and curses his creator. The monster reveals to Victor that Victor should have extinguished the spark of existence that he bestowed upon him.

The monster then headed for Geneva. On the way he saw a young girl slip into a stream and as he was rescuing her from drowning he was shot by a man who thought the monster was attacking the girl rather than helping her. This angered the monster and serves as a tipping point whereby the monster decides upon revenge. *"This was then the reward of my benevolence! I had saved a human being from destruction, and as a recompense I now writhed under the miserable pain of a wound which shattered the flesh and bone. The feelings of kindness and gentleness which I had entertained but a few moments before gave place to hellish rage and gnashing of teeth. Inflamed by pain, I vowed eternal hatred and vengeance to all mankind. But the agony of my wound overcame me; my pulses paused, and I fainted."*

As the monster neared Geneva, he explained, he saw William in the woods. When the monster heard the boy's father's last name was Frankenstein – the monster became enraged and strangled the boy with his bare hands. The monster took the picture of Caroline Frankenstein that William was holding and carefully placed it in the folds of the dress of a girl sleeping in the barn: Justine. This effectively framed her for the crime.

At this point, after revealing that he did indeed kill William, the monster begs Victor to create another monster to be his mate. The monster addresses Victor boldly and directly, reminding the reader of the relationship between the two. The monster's choice of words elicits a feeling in Victor – one that proves he believes he holds responsibility for the monster's actions.

Chapter 17: The monster tells Victor: *"You must create a female for me with whom I can live in the interchange of those sympathies necessary for my being. This you alone can do, and I demand it of you as a right which you must not refuse to concede."* At first Victor refuses, but he relates to the monster and he feels responsible for his desperate loneliness. The monster promises to go far away with his mate. The monster further promises he will no longer take lives if Victor grants this one request. Victor finally agrees and the monster is happy, but worried and skeptical Victor may change his mind.

The theme of nature and its power is present throughout Chapter 17. Nature humanizes both Victor and the monster. Victor seeks the cold summits of the Alps to hide away from the world where the monster references the colors and softness of the forest – the smells and colors of spring – to reveal himself to the world – to be **accepted** and reborn.

Paradise Lost discussion: The tenets of Milton's Paradise Lost should be reviewed or discussed. It is imperative for students to know Paradise Lost is an epic poem, written in the 17th Century, by John Milton. The poem is the story of the fall of man, the temptation of Adam and Eve and their subsequent loss of innocence, when they succumb to that temptation, and their ultimate expulsion from the Garden of Eden.

Encourage students to find past examples of this allusion. Great online resource for Paradise Lost include:
- https://www.mtholyoke.edu/courses/rschwart/hist257s02/students/Becky/paradise.html
- http://www.paradiselost.org/

Student "Critical Thinking Questions" answers should hit on the following notes:

Paradise Lost is about Adam and Eve and how they lose their place in the Garden of Eden. The story tells of the origin of Satan and his war waged against God – who banishes him from heaven. Satan, or Lucifer's, revenge leads him to cause man's downfall by tempting Eve to eat the forbidden fruit. After Eve eats the fruit she convinces Adam to do the same. Adam is bothered by the fact that she wants to disobey God, but he loves her and at her encouragement eats the fruit. Once they eat the fruit...they are no longer innocents. They have lost paradise. They now know lust and shame and distrust -- their thirst for knowledge led to their loss of innocence: their sentence - banishment from the Garden of Eden.

The monster doesn't know what fiction is and reads the poem as historical fact. He relates to the poem and is deeply affected. He longs for opportunity and to be accepted. The creature feels abandoned, helpless and without love and he describes his loss of innocence as the reason he committed the heinous acts he is responsible for.

The characters in Frankenstein are a collection of those in Paradise Lost. Victor Frankenstein is like Eve in the Garden of Eden in that they each do whatever it takes to gain knowledge. The monster, on the other hand, parallels Satan as they both desire to break free from their creators and receive a chance at making their own decisions.

In Chapter 15 of Frankenstein Shelley outright mentions Paradise Lost in order to establish a connection between the monster and Adam. The monster comes to grips with the fact that Victor abandoned him, thus he curses him and seeks revenge. The comparison to Satan is also evident in Chapter 10, when the monster states he feels like a "fallen angel, whom thou drivest from misjoy." Both Satan and the monster vow to destroy something good.

The monster also possesses similarities to the Satan from Paradise Lost. Both the monster and Satan were created to be divine and glorious beings: however, both are ultimately rejected by their creators. The major difference between Satan and the monster is the fact that Satan chose his fate, while the monster did not. Satan made a conscious decision to rebel against God, which directly led to his banishment, while the monster was cast aside because his creator did not like the way he looked.

*There is an alternate **Critical Thinking Questions** assignment for those not familiar with Paradise Lost.

Name: _____Date: _____

Chapters 15-17 Critical Thinking Questions

Analyze the following allusion within the novel text: *"But Paradise Lost excited different and far deeper emotions. I read it, as I had read the other volumes which had fallen into my hands, as a true history. It moved every feeling of wonder and awe that the picture of an omnipotent God warring with his creatures was capable of exciting. I often referred the several situations, as their similarity struck me, to my own. Like Adam, I was apparently united by no link to any other being in existence; but his state was far different from mine in every other respect. He had come forth from the hands of God a perfect creature, happy and prosperous, guarded by the especial care of his Creator; he was allowed to converse with and acquire knowledge from beings of a superior nature, but I was wretched, helpless, and alone. Many times I considered Satan as the fitter emblem of my condition, for often, like him, when I viewed the bliss of my protectors, the bitter gall of envy rose within me."*

_____

_____

_____

_____

_____

_____

_____

_____

_____

_____

_____

_____

_____

_____

_____

_____

_____

_____

_____

_____

_____

_____

_____

_____

_____

_____

_____

_____

_____

_____

_____

Name: _____ Date: _____

Chapters 15-17: Critical Thinking Questions – Alternate

1. What happens after the monster rescues the girl and how does this serve to further isolate the monster? _____

_____

_____

_____

_____

_____

_____

_____

_____

_____

_____

2. Remember that nature is important to the Romantic Movement – of which Gothic literature is a part. Discuss the presence and meaning of the power of nature within these chapters.

_____

_____

_____

_____

_____

_____

_____

_____

_____

_____

_____

3. Who is the monster's first victim and why? _____

_____

_____

_____

_____

_____

_____

_____

_____

_____

_____

Chapter 18: Victor begins to regret telling the monster he'd create a new, female creature. Victor decides he must go to England to study the research of a British philosopher in order to create the second creature – but first he must tell his father he is leaving.

Victor's father notices his son is still depressed. His father asks him if he is depressed over his impending marriage to Elizabeth. Victor assures him that he loves Elizabeth and really does want to marry her. His father suggests Elizabeth and Victor marry immediately; however, Victor wants to wait until he builds the mate for the monster. He tells his father he must first travel to England and his father agrees.

Victor and his father arrange a two-year-tour for Victor and his friend Henry Clerval. The two set off – arriving in London first.

Chapter 19: Victor is eager to free himself from his obligation to the monster. He and Henry journey to Oxford and Cumberland and Westmorland. He basically ditches Henry in Scotland and journeys to an isolated island to complete the task for which he came. He sets up a laboratory in a small cottage. He spends many hours working on his second monster.

Chapter 20: One night in his laboratory, Victor wonders whether he should finish his next creation quickly or give it up. He contemplates this second creature may be even more malignant than her mate and that they may loathe each other. He finds no relief in the promise that they will leave for the deserts of the New World as promised by the monster; because even there they could procreate. He wonders what will happen after he finishes his creation: *"I had been struck senseless by his fiendish threats; but now, for the first time, the wickedness of my promise burst upon me; I shuddered to think that future ages might curse me as their pest, whose selfishness had not hesitated to buy its own peace at the price, perhaps, of the existence of the whole human race."* He becomes distraught with the idea of a devil race.

Then, in true gothic form, Victor looks out of the window and in the moonlight he sees the monster, leering. With the knowledge that the monster has been stalking him, Victor ravenously rips to pieces the second creation. The creature outside howls in despair, but Victor merely walks out of the room and locks the door – vowing to himself never to engage in the act of creation again.

The monster is enraged and confronts Victor. They exchange venomous words and the monster swears to be with Victor on his wedding night.

The next night Victor receives a letter from Henry, who has grown tired of Scotland and wishes to resume their travels. So, in the dead of night, Victor piles all of his lab equipment and the remains of the second creature into a boat and rows out to sea. As weather and darkness play a role in Gothic literature – the passage where Victor heads to sea is haunting and a prime example of Gothic symbolism...particularly: *"Between two and three in the morning the moon rose; and I then, putting my basket aboard a little skiff, sailed out about four miles from the shore. The scene was perfectly solitary; a few boats were returning towards land, but I sailed away from them. I felt as if I was about the commission of a dreadful crime and avoided with shuddering anxiety any encounter with my fellow creatures. At one time the moon, which had before been clear, was suddenly overspread by a thick cloud, and I took advantage of the moment of darkness and cast my basket into the sea; I listened to the gurgling sound as it sank and then sailed away from the spot. The sky became clouded, but the air was pure, although chilled by the northeast breeze that was then rising. But it refreshed me and filled me with such agreeable sensations that I resolved to prolong my stay on the water, and fixing the rudder in a direct position, stretched myself at the bottom of the boat. Clouds hid the moon, everything was obscure, and I heard only the sound of the boat as its keel cut through the waves; the murmur lulled me, and in a short time I slept soundly. I do not know how long I remained in this situation, but when I awoke I found that the sun had already mounted considerably. The wind was high, and the waves continually threatened the safety of my little skiff."*

*This passage makes a great **Think, Pair, Share** or **Close Reading** activity.

Other Think, Pair, Share questions for this chapter could include:

- What is the significance of Victor not naming the monster? Victor created the monster but he does not give him a name. This is significant as the monster is not recognized as a being nor does Victor claim him as his own – his child, his son, his creation.
- Predict what you think will happen next. Be sure to look for evidence of foreshadowing. Think: how has the monster sought revenge before?

Teacher Notes:

Name: _____Date: _____

Chapters 18-20 Critical Thinking Questions

1. Select a passage from the novel, list the Gothic symbolism and explain its significance. _____
_____
_____
_____
_____
_____
_____
_____
_____
_____
_____

2. In Chapter 19 Victor contemplates: *"I enjoyed this scene, and yet my enjoyment was embittered both by the memory of the past and the anticipation of the future. I was formed for peaceful happiness. During my youthful days discontent never visited my mind, and if I was ever overcome by ennui, the sight of what is beautiful in nature or the study of what is excellent and sublime in the productions of man could always interest my heart and communicate elasticity to my spirits. But I am a blasted tree; the bolt has entered my soul; and I felt then that I should survive to exhibit what I shall soon cease to be—a miserable spectacle of wrecked humanity, pitiable to others and intolerable to myself."* Explain this passage. _____
_____
_____
_____
_____
_____
_____
_____
_____

3. Before you began reading Frankenstein what did you think the monster's name was? _____

4. **Think:** Victor doesn't give the monster a name. What does this do for the story? _____
_____
_____
_____
_____
_____
_____

5. What does it say for society that Victor does not give Frankenstein a name? _____
_____
_____
_____
_____
_____
_____
_____

Chapter 21: Victor has difficultly rowing back to shore and when he finally lands – exhausted – he is greeted by angry townspeople ready to arrest him for murder. They seize him and take him to the town magistrate, Mr. Kirwin. Mr. Kirwin believes that if Victor is the murderer he will react if he sees the dead body and, upon seeing the body, Victor reacts, not because he is the murderer, but because he sees the mark of the monster on the body of his dead friend Henry.

Victor is in agony and is carried from the room in convulsions. He is sick for two months – in his heart he feels he is indeed the murderer of William, Justine and now Henry. When he wakes from his fevered two months he discovers he is in prison and remembers the whole ordeal. He wishes for his own death. Mr. Kirwin, however, is compassionate and takes it upon himself to notify Victor's family of what's transpired. Victor's father visits and is able to take Victor home, as it has been discovered that Victor could not have been the murderer because he was on the island where he was staying when the murder took place.

Chapter 22: On their way back to Geneva, Victor and his father visit Paris to give Victor time to rest. Victor receives a letter from Elizabeth who inquires if he is having second thoughts about their wedding. She wonders if this is the cause of his illness. He is reminded of the monster's threat, but resolves to fight back. He knows that only one will survive an encounter – either he or the monster – but either way – an end will finally come.

Love for Elizabeth overtakes him and once again allusion enters Shelley's writing: *"Sweet and beloved Elizabeth! I read and reread her letter, and some softened feelings stole into my heart and dared to whisper paradisiacal dreams of love and joy; but the apple was already eaten, and the angel's arm bared to drive me from all hope. Yet I would die to make her happy. If the monster executed his threat, death was inevitable; yet, again, I considered whether my marriage would hasten my fate. My destruction might indeed arrive a few months sooner, but if my torturer should suspect that I postponed it, influenced by his menaces, he would surely find other and perhaps more dreadful means of revenge."* Point out that this passage also alludes to Paradise Lost and draw a comparison again for your students.

He decides to marry Elizabeth immediately and tells her he has a secret he will reveal after they are married. As the wedding approaches, Victor grows nervous of his impending encounter with the monster. The wedding finally takes place – after which, he and Elizabeth depart for the family cottage.

Discuss foreshadowing of the following passage: *"The sun sank beneath the horizon as we landed, and as I touched the shore I felt those cares and fears revive which soon were to clasp me and cling to me forever."*

Chapters 21-22 Critical Thinking Questions

1. Elaborate on the foreshowing in the following passage: *"The sun sank beneath the horizon as we landed, and as I touched the shore I felt those cares and fears revive which soon were to clasp me and cling to me forever."*

_____
_____
_____
_____
_____
_____
_____
_____

2. What are the consequences when one doesn't take responsibility for ones actions? Please relate this question to your life and to the events of the novel Frankenstein. _____

_____
_____
_____
_____
_____
_____
_____
_____

3. Romantic/Gothic literature commonly uses nature as an omnipotent force. Site three examples from these Chapters where Shelley uses nature as such a force. _____

_____
_____
_____
_____
_____
_____
_____
_____

4. Predict what you think will happen next in the novel. _____

_____
_____
_____
_____
_____
_____

5. On what do you base your prediction? _____

_____
_____
_____
_____
_____
_____

Chapter 23: The newlyweds walk around and enjoy nature and the fleeting light. As they retire to the cottage a great and violent wind rises. Victor sends Elizabeth to bed and goes to check the cottage one last time. (This is a perfect point to tie-in modern horror movies. Why does the protagonist always leave the girl alone when certain danger looms?) Victor hears a scream, races to the bedroom and finds Elizabeth dead. This is the climax of the novel. At this point, everything is taken from Victor by the monster – his family, his best friend and his faith in science. The only thing left is his hatred for the monster he created. With Elizabeth gone, the most important and human part of his life, he is reduced to the monster he created, complete with the same thirst for revenge exhibited by the monster.

This climax has been foreshadowed throughout the novel. The murder of Elizabeth was sealed and commenced when Victor decided not to create a mate for the monster -- as he previously promised. Victor left the monster alone, isolated and without a partner and that is how the monster left Victor with this final murder.

Victor is consumed with grief. He returns home to tell his father – who dies with the culmination of all of the tragic news. Elizabeth was like a daughter to the senior Mr. Frankenstein, more than a daughter and she had cared for him and loved him – thus the elderly man dies under the horrors that accumulated around him.

Chapter 24: Everything is destroyed. Victor leaves Geneva to track the monster. The monster, in turn, taunts him – leaving clues. Victor's pursuit takes him North to the snow and ice. Here the story comes full circle as Victor meets Captain Walton. He tells his story and enlists Walton to continue his quest after he dies.

Walton, in Continuation: The narrative now returns to Walton – who continues the story in the form of letters to his sister. He writes his sister of the danger he is in as he and his crew are surrounded by ice. The crew begs to return to England if they break out of the ice. Walton tries to convince his men that they want the honor of their scientific discovery for the benefit of mankind. They are motivated, but only for a short while. Finally, Walton relents. Walton is disappointed. He wants the glory.

Victor will not abandon his quest; however, he is sick and he dies. Walton hears a strange noise coming from the room where Victor's dead body lay. He discovers the monster weeping over his creator. The monster begins to tell his tale – one of self-loathing and remorse. *"No guilt, no mischief, no malignity, no misery, can be found comparable to mine. When I run over the frightful catalogue of my sins, I cannot believe that I am the same creature whose thoughts were once filled with sublime and transcendent visions of the beauty and the majesty of goodness. But it is even so; the fallen angel becomes a malignant devil. Yet even that enemy of God and man had friends and associates in his desolation; I am alone."*

What lesson can be learned in the monster's words: *"You, who call Frankenstein your friend, seem to have a knowledge of my crimes and his misfortunes. But in the detail which he gave you of them he could not sum up the hours and months of misery which I endured wasting in impotent passions. For while I destroyed his hopes, I did not satisfy my own desires. They were forever ardent and craving; still I desired love and fellowship, and I was still spurned. Was there no injustice in this? Am I to be thought the only criminal, when all humankind sinned against me? Why do you not hate Felix, who drove his friend from his door with contumely? Why do you not execrate the rustic who sought to destroy the saviour of his child? Nay, these are virtuous and immaculate beings! I, the miserable and the abandoned, am an abortion, to be spurned at, and kicked, and trampled on. Even now my blood boils at the recollection of this injustice."*

The monster then leaves the ship and floats off into the darkness on a cold block of ice. In this final chapter, both Frankenstein and the monster compare themselves to Satan. The novel ends leaving the reader feeling sorry for the monster, as he never intended to be evil or bad. When the monster weeps over his creator – it is poignant. The monster feels a regret that Victor never felt. In the end Victor is the pursuer.

Teacher Notes:

Name: _____ Date: _____

Chapters 23-24 and Walton, in Continuation Critical Thinking Questions

1. In Chapter 23, Victor says: "Oh! Peace, peace, my love," replied I: "this night, and all will be safe: but this night is dreadful, very dreadful." What is Victor referring to? _____
_____
_____
_____
_____
_____
_____

2. Please use sensory detail to describe the climax of the novel. _____
_____
_____
_____
_____
_____
_____
_____

3. In Chapter 24, why does Victor kiss the earth? _____
_____
_____
_____
_____
_____
_____

4. Analyze the end of the novel, assert an opinion regarding the final scene and support your answer with details. _____
_____
_____
_____
_____
_____
_____
_____
_____
_____
_____
_____
_____
_____
_____
_____
_____

Vocabulary Acquisition

1. Vocabulary Notebook: Have students keep a vocabulary notebook.   Answer the following questions about each word.
- Word – with the page and text containing the word
- Word used in context (the original sentence)
- Predicted definition (you guess what the words mean)
- Dictionary Definition
- Antonyms
- A way to remember the word (symbol, association)

AP Frankenstein Vocabulary List

This list is comprised of words students need to know for this novel, the AP test and college.

1. satiate
2. ardent
3. conciliating
4. evinced
5. ardour
6. fastidious
7. marvelous (not synonym for amazing)
8. singular (not in the math world)
9. caprice
10. vehement
11. palpable
12. spurn
13. abhorred
14. base (again, you need to find something besides math, science or construction)
15. abject
16. infamy

Footnoted words on the bottom of the <u>One Summer in Geneva 1816</u> Edition

Letters:
Endeavor (v): to exert oneself to do or effect something.
Suppliant (n): petitioner.
Embarkation (n): the act of beginning

Chapter 1:
Syndics: (n): a civil magistrate justice.
Indefatigable (adj): incapable of being tried out.
Bestowed (v): presented as a gift.
Reverential (adj): characterized by a feeling of awe.

Chapter 2:
Sepulcher (n): tomb, grave or burial place.
Vehement (adj): zealous, with strong emotions
Beneficence (n): the doing of good.
Impediments (n): obstruction, hindrance.

Chapter 3:
Prognosticated (v): to forecast or predict.
Appertaining (v): belonging to or relating to.
Affirmative (adj): positive, not negative.
Chimera (n): a mythological, fire-breathing monster.

Chapter 4:
Pedantry (n): one who makes a show of being knowledgeable.
Infallible (adj): incapable of error.
Inconceivable (adj): impossible to comprehend.

Chapter 5:
Countenance (n): a face or facial expression.
Specter (n): apparition, ghost.
Convalescence (n): a gradual return to health.

Chapter 6:
Perambulations (v): to inspect on foot.

Chapter 7:
Agitation (n): extreme emotional disturbance.
Alterations (n): the act or procedure of modifying.
Promontory (n): a projecting part.
Impenetrable (adj): dense and impassable.
Precipices (n): a steep rock face or cliff.
Alleviate (v): lessen or relieve.
Ingratitude (n): ungratefulness
Acquitted (v): freed or cleared.

Chapter 8
Ignominious (adj): marked by shame or disgrace.
Aquit (v): Free as from a criminal charge.
Benevolent (adj): Well meaning and kind.
Approbation (noun): Act of approving officially.
Manacled (v): hands confined with a device called a manacle.
Obdurate (adj): stubbornly refusing to change one's opinion.
Ignominy (n): public shame or disgrace.
Perdition (n): a state of eternal punishment or damnation.
Eloquence (n): persuasiveness or expressiveness.

Chapter 9
Complacency (n): a feeling of contentment especially with unawareness of danger.
Malice (n): hatred, spite or cruelty.
Abhorrence (n): hate, detestation.
Omnipotent (n): an agency or force of unlimited power.
Pallid (adj): lacking in color or sparkle.
Oblivion (n): the state or condition of being unknown or forgotten.

Chapter 10:
perpendicularity (n): exactly upright or standing at right angles.
Transversely (adv): adverse or diagonally.
Dissoluble (adj): able to be dissolved, loosened or disconnected.
Annihilation (v): to completely destroy.
Commiserate (v): express or feel sympathy or pity.

Chapter 11:
Savory (adj): morally exemplary.
Innumerable (adv): to many to be numbered.
Purloined (v): to steal or violate a trust.
Demeanor (n): outward behavior or bearing.
Incommoded (v): inconvenience.
Monotonous (adj): lacking in varied and interest.

Chapter 12
Venerable (adj): accorded a great deal of respect.
Enigmatic (adj): difficult to understand or interpret or mysterious.
Despondence (n): feeling hopeless and downcast.
Mortification (n): a feeling of shame or humiliation.

Chapter 13
Ravished (v): seize or carry off by force.
Rapturously (adj): filled with joy or ecstatic.
Stupendous (adj): extremely impressive.

Chapter 14
Affluence (n): an abundant flow or property.
Dominions (n): sovereign authority. The power or right of controlling.
Asylum (n): an institution for the care of people.
Tyrannical (adj): exercising power in a cruel or arbitrary way.

Chapter 15
Lament (n): a passionate expression of grief.
Massacring (v): deliberately and violently kill.
Patriarchal (adj): ruled by a patriarch or male.
Hideousness (adj): repulsive, especially to sight.

Chapter 16
Gesticulations (n): an expressive gesture showing strong feelings.
Combustibles (adj): capable of igniting or burning.
Succor (n): assistance in time of hardship.
Visage (n): a person's face.
Recompense (v): make a mess for loss or harm.
Augmented (adv): having made greater in size or value.
Ingratitude (n): forgetful or poor return for kindness.
Stupendous (adj): extremely impressive.
Malignity (n): intense ill will or hatred. Great malice.
Requisition (n): a formal act of calling one to action.

Chapter 17
Insurmountable (adj): too great to overcome.
Undulations (n): a rising or falling in waves.

Chapter 18
Repugnance (n): intense disgust.
Devouring (v): eat quickly or hungrily.
Conjure (v): make appear unexpectedly.
Solemnization (v): to celebrate or observe with dignity.
Acquiesced (v): accept something reluctantly but without protest.
Sedulous (adj): showing dedication.
Meandering (v): follow a winding course.
Eminently (adv): to a high degree.

Chapter 19
Picturesque (adj): charming or quaint.
Debasing (v): reduce in quality or value.
Congenial (adj): pleasant because of personality.
Pittance (n): a very small or inadequate amount of money as payment.

Chapter 20
Profundity (n): deep insight.
Irresolution (adj): uncertainty in how to act.
Barbarously (adj): lacking culture or refinement.
Solitary (adj): existing without others, sole or alone.

Chapter 21
Squalidness (n): state of being dirty.
Repugnance (n): intense disgust.
Melancholy (n): a deep, pensive long lasting sadness.
Assizes (n): a periodic court session.
Laudanum (n): a form of opium.

Chapter 22
Indefatigable (adj): persisting tirelessly.
Incoherent (adj): unclear or confusing.
Inclination (n): a person's natural tendency to feel a certain way.
Emaciated (v): to become painfully thin.
Demeanor (n): outward behavior.

Chapter 23
Contemplated (v): look at thoughtfully.
Conjecture (n): interpretation.
Incredulous (adj): unwilling or unable to believe something.
Physiognomy (n): the ability of developing character from outward appearance.

Chapter 24
Vengeance (n) punishment inflicted with force.
Adjuration (n): an urging or advising.
Audible (adj): able to be heard.
Toilsome (adj): involving hard work.
Disencumbered (v): to relieve from hardship.
Demoniacal (adj): possessed.

Differentiated Activities

Chapter-by-Chapter

Close Reading or Fluency Passages

Chapter-by-Chapter Close Reading and Fluency Passages

Close Reading provides teachers with a resource that promotes careful analysis of text while building 21st Century skills of critical thinking, collaboration, and communication. Fluency practice helps struggling readers become proficient.

The following passages are taken directly from Mary Shelley's <u>Frankenstein</u>. In classes containing multi-level students the passages can be differentiated so that average to advanced students participate in a Close Reading activity while struggling and/or at risk students can practice reading fluency. The Close activities are further differentiated with a template for student to fill out if they are in the process of learning to analyze literature. The template enables students who are working towards analytical skill proficiency to gain confidence in their writing and higher order thinking skills while participating in the assignment.

INSTRUCTIONS: Fluency:
The passages are one minute timed readings.
1. Pair students
2. Provide a stopwatch, a watch with a second hand or let them use their phones
3. Provide two copies of each passage per pair
4. Student One will read the passage while Student Two times the reading and marks mistakes
5. Mistakes will be marked by circling words mispronounced or skipped
6. When time is up, Student Two will make a notation where Student One stopped reading; however, Student One should be allowed to finish the entire passage
7. Student One will now time while Student Two reads
8. Students will calculate Combined Words Per Minute (CWPM) by subtracting the number of errors from the total number of words read

INSTRUCTIONS: Close Reading General
A Close Reading is just reading a specific and limited passage and analyzing it under a magnifying glass – the finer the detail the better. The analysis includes points of style and the reader's reaction to the passage. Close reading is essential for honing one's skills for further and greater literary analysis.

Close reading helps foster fundamental skills, especially in the Common Core State Standards classroom, that enable students to learn to read text and arrive at their own conclusions and then articulate these conclusions along with evidence from the text.

INSTRUCTIONS: Close Reading Level 1:
Students will read and annotate each passage and then return to the passage and fill out the *Close Reading Template*. Share **Close Reading Student Instructions** and then let students read and analyze.

INSTRUCTIONS: Close Reading Level 2:
Students will read and analyze the given passage and then organize their thoughts in essay form – paragraph by paragraph.

Close Reading Student Instructions

This passage is for use as a Close Reading. A Close Reading is actually a careful rereading of a passage. The objective of this assignment is to analyze the passage in extreme detail. Read the passage, making notes and annotations regarding points of style and your reaction to what the author says and how she says it and then communicate your ideas in an analysis of the work. The goal is to form your own opinions and thoughts from your own observations. Thus, the more closely you observe the more precise and original your ideas will be. So read and analyze carefully and form your own opinions.

When you read, it is imperative to do thoughtful annotating. Annotating just means underlying or highlighting key words and phrases and taking notes in the margins. Anything that seems out of the ordinary or significant should be noted.

When you come to conclusions about the reading, write them down in paragraph form – as if you are organizing an essay. The following questions are to be used as a guide only – as a starting point – to help you question the passage and analyze it thoroughly.

1. What are your first impressions of the passage, including:
   • What stands out? What did reading the passage make you think of?
   • What did you notice first?
   • What mood does the passage create?
   • Are there any contradictions?

2. What did you notice about the vocabulary and diction?
   • Which words stand out?
   • What about the diction? Why are certain words chosen over others?
   • Do any words seem odd to you?
   • Are there any unstated connotations within the text?
   • Are there any words you don't know or understand?

3. What is the point of view of the passage?
   • How does the passage make you think or react about the characters?
   • Are there any specific physical descriptions that stand out?
   • Are any of your senses peeked? For example, are there colors or sounds you find particularly appealing?
   • Does anyone speak in the passage? If so, who and to whom?

4. What about the actual writing?
   • What do you picture when you read the passage?
   • Is the passage the same or different from the rest of the novel?
   • Is there a standard sentence rhythm?
   • What types of writing are in the passage – narrative, descriptive, etc.
   • Are there patterns in the text – contradictions, repetitions, similarities?
   • Are there any contradictions, or paradoxes, within the writing that seem out of place within the context of the novel?

5. Is there symbolism in the passage?
   • Are there any allusions in the passage? If so, what do they reference and why?
   • Does the author use allegories?
   • Do objects represent things other than what they actually are?

Name: _____ Date: _____

Close Reading Template

Observation 1: First Impression	
Observation 2: Vocabulary and/or Diction	
Observation 3: What stands out about the writing?	
Observation 4: Symbolism and other literary devices	

Letters 1-4 Close Reading
From Letter 2

I cannot describe to you my sensations on the near prospect of my	13
undertaking. It is impossible to communicate to you a conception of the	25
trembling sensation, half pleasurable and half fearful, with which I am	36
preparing to depart. I am going to unexplored regions, to "the land of mist and	51
snow," but I shall kill no albatross; therefore do not be alarmed for my safety	67
or if I should come back to you as worn and woeful as the "Ancient Mariner."	73
You will smile at my allusion, but I will disclose a secret. I have often	88
attributed my attachment to, my passionate enthusiasm for, the dangerous	98
mysteries of ocean to that production of the most imaginative of modern poets.	111
There is something at work in my soul which I do not understand. I am	126
practically industrious—painstaking, a workman to execute with perseverance	135
and labour—but besides this there is a love for the marvellous, a belief in the	151
marvellous, intertwined in all my projects, which hurries me out of the	163
common pathways of men, even to the wild sea and unvisited regions I am	177
about to explore. But to return to dearer considerations. Shall I meet you	190
again, after having traversed immense seas, and returned by the most	202
southern cape of Africa or America? I dare not expect such success, yet I	216
cannot bear to look on the reverse of the picture. Continue for the present to	231
write to me by every opportunity: I may receive your letters on some occasions	244
when I need them most to support my spirits. I love you very tenderly.	258
Remember me with affection, should you never hear from me again.	269

Total Words Read: _____

Minus Errors: _____

CWPM: _____ _____

Name: _____ Date: _____

Chapter 1 Close Reading

When my father returned from Milan, he found playing with me in the hall	14
of our villa a child fairer than pictured cherub—a creature who seemed to	28
shed radiance from her looks and whose form and motions were lighter than	41
the chamois of the hills. The apparition was soon explained. With his	53
permission my mother prevailed on her rustic guardians to yield their charge	65
to her. They were fond of the sweet orphan. Her presence had seemed a	79
blessing to them, but it would be unfair to her to keep her in poverty and want	96
when Providence afforded her such powerful protection. They consulted their	106
village priest, and the result was that Elizabeth Lavenza became the inmate of	119
my parents' house—my more than sister—the beautiful and adored	130
companion of all my occupations and my pleasures.	139
Everyone loved Elizabeth. The passionate and almost reverential	147
attachment with which all regarded her became, while I shared it, my pride	160
and my delight. On the evening previous to her being brought to my home, my	175
mother had said playfully, "I have a pretty present for my Victor—tomorrow he	189
shall have it." And when, on the morrow, she presented Elizabeth to me as her	204
promised gift, I, with childish seriousness, interpreted her words literally and	215
looked upon Elizabeth as mine—mine to protect, love, and cherish. All praises	228
bestowed on her I received as made to a possession of my own. We called each	244
other familiarly by the name of cousin. No word, no expression could body	257
forth the kind of relation in which she stood to me—my more than sister,	272
since till death she was to be mine only.	281

Total Words Read: _____

Minus Errors: _____

CWPM: _____ _____

Chapter 2 Close Reading

My temper was sometimes violent, and my passions vehement; but by	11
some law in my temperature they were turned not towards childish pursuits	23
but to an eager desire to learn, and not to learn all things indiscriminately. I	38
confess that neither the structure of languages, nor the code of governments,	50
nor the politics of various states possessed attractions for me. It was the	63
secrets of heaven and earth that I desired to learn; and whether it was the	78
outward substance of things or the inner spirit of nature and the mysterious	91
soul of man that occupied me, still my inquiries were directed to the	104
metaphysical, or in its highest sense, the physical secrets of the world.	116
Meanwhile Clerval occupied himself, so to speak, with the moral relations	127
of things. The busy stage of life, the virtues of heroes, and the actions of men	143
were his theme; and his hope and his dream was to become one among those	158
whose names are recorded in story as the gallant and adventurous	169
benefactors of our species. The saintly soul of Elizabeth shone like a shrine-	182
dedicated lamp in our peaceful home. Her sympathy was ours; her smile, her	195
soft voice, the sweet glance of her celestial eyes, were ever there to bless and	210
animate us. She was the living spirit of love to soften and attract; I might have	226
become sullen in my study, rought through the ardour of my nature, but that	240
she was there to subdue me to a semblance of her own gentleness. And	253
Clerval—could aught ill entrench on the noble spirit of Clerval? Yet he might	267
not have been so perfectly humane, so thoughtful in his generosity, so full of	271
kindness and tenderness amidst his passion for adventurous exploit, had she	282
not unfolded to him the real loveliness of beneficence and made the doing	295
good the end and aim of his soaring ambition.	304

Total Words Read: _____
Minus Errors: _____
CWPM: _____ _____

Name: _____ Date: _____

Chapter 3 Close Reading

The day of my departure at length arrived. Clerval spent the last evening	13
with us. He had endeavoured to persuade his father to permit him to	26
accompany me and to become my fellow student, but in vain. His father was a	41
narrow-minded trader and saw idleness and ruin in the aspirations and	53
ambition of his son. Henry deeply felt the misfortune of being debarred from a	67
liberal education. He said little, but when he spoke I read in his kindling eye	82
and in his animated glance a restrained but firm resolve not to be chained to	97
the miserable details of commerce.	102
We sat late. We could not tear ourselves away from each other nor	115
persuade ourselves to say the word "Farewell!" It was said, and we retired	128
under the pretence of seeking repose, each fancying that the other was	140
deceived; but when at morning's dawn I descended to the carriage which was	153
to convey me away, they were all there—my father again to bless me, Clerval	168
to press my hand once more, my Elizabeth to renew her entreaties that I	182
would write often and to bestow the last feminine attentions on her playmate	195
and friend.	197
I threw myself into the chaise that was to convey me away and indulged in	212
the most melancholy reflections. I, who had ever been surrounded by amiable	224
companions, continually engaged in endeavouring to bestow mutual	232
pleasure—I was now alone. In the university whither I was going I must form	247
my own friends and be my own protector. My life had hitherto been	260
remarkably secluded and domestic, and this had given me invincible	270
repugnance to new countenances. I loved my brothers, Elizabeth, and Clerval;	281
these were "old familiar faces," but I believed myself totally unfitted for the	294
company of strangers.	297

Total Words Read: _____

Minus Errors: _____

CWPM: _____ _____

Name: _____ Date: _____

Chapter 4 Close Reading

When I found so astonishing a power placed within my hands, I hesitated	13
a long time concerning the manner in which I should employ it. Although I	27
possessed the capacity of bestowing animation, yet to prepare a frame for the	40
reception of it, with all its intricacies of fibres, muscles, and veins, still	53
remained a work of inconceivable difficulty and labour. I doubted at first	65
whether I should attempt the creation of a being like myself, or one of simpler	80
organization; but my imagination was too much exalted by my first success to	93
permit me to doubt of my ability to give life to an animal as complex and	109
wonderful as man. The materials at present within my command hardly	120
appeared adequate to so arduous an undertaking, but I doubted not that I	133
should ultimately succeed. I prepared myself for a multitude of reverses; my	145
operations might be incessantly baffled, and at last my work be imperfect, yet	158
when I considered the improvement which every day takes place in science	170
and mechanics, I was encouraged to hope my present attempts would at least	183
lay the foundations of future success. Nor could I consider the magnitude and	196
complexity of my plan as any argument of its impracticability. It was with	209
these feelings that I began the creation of a human being. As the minuteness	223
of the parts formed a great hindrance to my speed, I resolved, contrary to my	238
first intention, to make the being of a gigantic stature, that is to say, about	253
eight feet in height, and proportionably large. After having formed this	264
determination and having spent some months in successfully collecting and	274
arranging my materials, I began.	279
No one can conceive the variety of feelings which bore me onwards, like a	293
hurricane, in the first enthusiasm of success. Life and death appeared to me	309
ideal bounds, which I should first break through, and pour a torrent of light	323
into our dark world.	327

Total Words Read: _____
Minus Errors: _____
CWPM: _____ _____

Name: _____ Date: _____

Chapter 5 Close Reading

It was on a dreary night of November that I beheld the accomplishment of	14
my toils. With an anxiety that almost amounted to agony, I collected the	27
instruments of life around me, that I might infuse a spark of being into the	42
lifeless thing that lay at my feet. It was already one in the morning; the rain	58
pattered dismally against the panes, and my candle was nearly burnt out,	70
when, by the glimmer of the half-extinguished light, I saw the dull yellow eye	86
of the creature open; it breathed hard, and a convulsive motion agitated its	99
limbs.	100
How can I describe my emotions at this catastrophe, or how delineate the	113
wretch whom with such infinite pains and care I had endeavoured to form?	126
His limbs were in proportion, and I had selected his features as beautiful.	139
Beautiful! Great God! His yellow skin scarcely covered the work of muscles	151
and arteries beneath; his hair was of a lustrous black, and flowing; his teeth	165
of a pearly whiteness; but these luxuriances only formed a more horrid	177
contrast with his watery eyes, that seemed almost of the same colour as the	191
dun-white sockets in which they were set, his shrivelled complexion and	203
straight black lips.	206

Total Words Read: _____

Minus Errors: _____

CWPM: _____ _____

Chapter 6 Close Reading

"One by one, her brothers and sister died; and her mother, with the	13
exception of her neglected daughter, was left childless. The conscience of the	25
woman was troubled; she began to think that the deaths of her favourites was	39
a judgement from heaven to chastise her partiality. She was a Roman	51
Catholic; and I believe her confessor confirmed the idea which she had	63
conceived. Accordingly, a few months after your departure for Ingolstadt,	72
Justine was called home by her repentant mother. Poor girl! She wept when	85
she quitted our house; she was much altered since the death of my aunt; grief	100
had given softness and a winning mildness to her manners, which had before	113
been remarkable for vivacity. Nor was her residence at her mother's house of a	127
nature to restore her gaiety. The poor woman was very vacillating in her	140
repentance. She sometimes begged Justine to forgive her unkindness, but	150
much oftener accused her of having caused the deaths of her brothers and	163
sister. Perpetual fretting at length threw Madame Moritz into a decline, which	175
at first increased her irritability, but she is now at peace for ever. She died on	191
the first approach of cold weather, at the beginning of this last winter. Justine	205
has just returned to us; and I assure you I love her tenderly. She is very clever	222
and gentle, and extremely pretty; as I mentioned before, her mien and her	235
expression continually remind me of my dear aunt.	243
"I must say also a few words to you, my dear cousin, of little darling	258
William. I wish you could see him; he is very tall of his age, with sweet	274
laughing blue eyes, dark eyelashes, and curling hair. When he smiles, two	276
little dimples appear on each cheek, which are rosy with health. He has	289
already had one or two little WIVES, but Louisa Biron is his favourite, a pretty	307
little girl of five years of age.	314

Total Words Read: _____
Minus Errors: _____
CWPM: _____ _____

Name: _____ Date: _____

Chapter 7 Close Reading

I remained motionless. The thunder ceased; but the rain still continued,	11
and the scene was enveloped in an impenetrable darkness. I revolved in my	24
mind the events which I had until now sought to forget: the whole train of my	40
progress toward the creation; the appearance of the works of my own hands at	54
my bedside; its departure. Two years had now nearly elapsed since the night	67
on which he first received life; and was this his first crime? Alas! I had turned	83
loose into the world a depraved wretch, whose delight was in carnage and	96
misery; had he not murdered my brother?	103
No one can conceive the anguish I suffered during the remainder of the	115
night, which I spent, cold and wet, in the open air. But I did not feel the	132
inconvenience of the weather; my imagination was busy in scenes of evil and	145
despair. I considered the being whom I had cast among mankind, and	157
endowed with the will and power to effect purposes of horror, such as the deed	172
which he had now done, nearly in the light of my own vampire, my own spirit	188
let loose from the grave, and forced to destroy all that was dear to me.	203

Total Words Read: _____

Minus Errors: _____

CWPM: _____ _____

Name: _____ Date: _____

Chapter 8 Close Reading

And on the morrow Justine died. Elizabeth's heart-rending eloquence failed	11
to move the judges from their settled conviction in the criminality of the	24
saintly sufferer. My passionate and indignant appeals were lost upon them.	36
And when I received their cold answers and heard the harsh, unfeeling	48
reasoning of these men, my purposed avowal died away on my lips. Thus I	62
might proclaim myself a madman, but not revoke the sentence passed upon	74
my wretched victim. She perished on the scaffold as a murderess!	85
From the tortures of my own heart, I turned to contemplate the deep and	99
voiceless grief of my Elizabeth. This also was my doing! And my father's woe,	113
and the desolation of that late so smiling home all was the work of my thrice-	129
accursed hands! Ye weep, unhappy ones, but these are not your last tears!	142
Again shall you raise the funeral wail, and the sound of your lamentations	155
shall again and again be heard! Frankenstein, your son, your kinsman, your	167
early, much-loved friend; he who would spend each vital drop of blood for your	182
sakes, who has no thought nor sense of joy except as it is mirrored also in	198
your dear countenances, who would fill the air with blessings and spend his	211
life in serving you—he bids you weep, to shed countless tears; happy beyond	225
his hopes, if thus inexorable fate be satisfied, and if the destruction pause	238
before the peace of the grave have succeeded to your sad torments!	250
Thus spoke my prophetic soul, as, torn by remorse, horror, and despair, I	263
beheld those I loved spend vain sorrow upon the graves of William and	276
Justine, the first hapless victims to my unhallowed arts.	285

Total Words Read: _____
Minus Errors: _____
CWPM: _____ _____

Name: _____ Date: _____

Chapter 9 Close Reading

At these moments I wept bitterly and wished that peace would revisit my	13
mind only that I might afford them consolation and happiness. But that could	26
not be. Remorse extinguished every hope. I had been the author of unalterable	39
evils, and I lived in daily fear lest the monster whom I had created should	54
perpetrate some new wickedness. I had an obscure feeling that all was not	67
over and that he would still commit some signal crime, which by its enormity	81
should almost efface the recollection of the past. There was always scope for	94
fear so long as anything I loved remained behind. My abhorrence of this fiend	108
cannot be conceived. When I thought of him I gnashed my teeth, my eyes	122
became inflamed, and I ardently wished to extinguish that life which I had so	136
thoughtlessly bestowed. When I reflected on his crimes and malice, my hatred	148
and revenge burst all bounds of moderation. I would have made a pilgrimage	161
to the highest peak of the Andes, could I when there have precipitated him to	176
their base. I wished to see him again, that I might wreak the utmost extent of	192
abhorrence on his head and avenge the deaths of William and Justine. Our	205
house was the house of mourning. My father's health was deeply shaken by	218
the horror of the recent events. Elizabeth was sad and desponding; she no	231
longer took delight in her ordinary occupations; all pleasure seemed to her	243
sacrilege toward the dead; eternal woe and tears she then thought was the	256
just tribute she should pay to innocence so blasted and destroyed. She was no	270
longer that happy creature who in earlier youth wandered with me on the	283
banks of the lake and talked with ecstasy of our future prospects. The first of	298
those sorrows which are sent to wean us from the earth had visited her, and	313
its dimming influence quenched her dearest smiles.	320

Total Words Read: _____

Minus Errors: _____

CWPM: _____ _____

Name: _____ Date: _____

Chapter 10 Close Reading

"How can I move thee? Will no entreaties cause thee to turn a favourable eye	15
upon thy creature, who implores thy goodness and compassion? Believe me,	26
Frankenstein, I was benevolent; my soul glowed with love and humanity; but	38
am I not alone, miserably alone? You, my creator, abhor me; what hope can I	53
gather from your fellow creatures, who owe me nothing? They spurn and hate	66
me. The desert mountains and dreary glaciers are my refuge. I have wandered	79
here many days; the caves of ice, which I only do not fear, are a dwelling to	96
me, and the only one which man does not grudge. These bleak skies I hail, for	112
they are kinder to me than your fellow beings. If the multitude of mankind	126
knew of my existence, they would do as you do, and arm themselves for my	141
destruction. Shall I not then hate them who abhor me? I will keep no terms	156
with my enemies. I am miserable, and they shall share my wretchedness. Yet	169
it is in your power to recompense me, and deliver them from an evil which it	175
only remains for you to make so great, that not only you and your family, but	191
thousands of others, shall be swallowed up in the whirlwinds of its rage. Let	205
your compassion be moved, and do not disdain me. Listen to my tale; when	219
you have heard that, abandon or commiserate me, as you shall judge that I	233
deserve. But hear me. The guilty are allowed, by human laws, bloody as they	247
are, to speak in their own defence before they are condemned. Listen to me,	261
Frankenstein. You accuse me of murder, and yet you would, with a satisfied	274
conscience, destroy your own creature. Oh, praise the eternal justice of man!	286
Yet I ask you not to spare me; listen to me, and then, if you can, and if you	308
will, destroy the work of your hands."	315

Total Words Read: _____

Minus Errors: _____

CWPM: _____ _____

Name: _____ Date: _____

Chapter 11 Close Reading

"One day, when I was oppressed by cold, I found a fire which had been left	16
by some wandering beggars, and was overcome with delight at the warmth I	29
experienced from it. In my joy I thrust my hand into the live embers, but	44
quickly drew it out again with a cry of pain. How strange, I thought, that the	60
same cause should produce such opposite effects! I examined the materials of	72
the fire, and to my joy found it to be composed of wood. I quickly collected	88
some branches, but they were wet and would not burn. I was pained at this	103
and sat still watching the operation of the fire. The wet wood which I had	118
placed near the heat dried and itself became inflamed. I reflected on this, and	132
by touching the various branches, I discovered the cause and busied myself in	145
collecting a great quantity of wood, that I might dry it and have a plentiful	160
supply of fire. When night came on and brought sleep with it, I was in the	176
greatest fear lest my fire should be extinguished. I covered it carefully with dry	189
wood and leaves and placed wet branches upon it; and then, spreading my	202
cloak, I lay on the ground and sank into sleep.	212

Total Words Read: _____

Minus Errors: _____

CWPM: _____ _____

Name: _____ Date: _____

Chapter 12 Close Reading

"My thoughts now became more active, and I longed to discover the	12
motives and feelings of these lovely creatures; I was inquisitive to know why	25
Felix appeared so miserable and Agatha so sad. I thought (foolish wretch!) that	38
it might be in my power to restore happiness to these deserving people. When	52
I slept or was absent, the forms of the venerable blind father, the gentle	66
Agatha, and the excellent Felix flitted before me. I looked upon them as	79
superior beings who would be the arbiters of my future destiny. I formed in	93
my imagination a thousand pictures of presenting myself to them, and their	105
reception of me. I imagined that they would be disgusted, until, by my gentle	120
demeanour and conciliating words, I should first win their favour and	131
afterwards their love.	134
"These thoughts exhilarated me and led me to apply with fresh ardour to	147
the acquiring the art of language. My organs were indeed harsh, but supple;	160
and although my voice was very unlike the soft music of their tones, yet I	175
pronounced such words as I understood with tolerable ease. It was as the ass	189
and the lap-dog; yet surely the gentle ass whose intentions were affectionate,	202
although his manners were rude, deserved better treatment than blows and	213
execration.	214
"The pleasant showers and genial warmth of spring greatly altered the	225
aspect of the earth. Men who before this change seemed to have been hid in	240
caves dispersed themselves and were employed in various arts of cultivation.	251
The birds sang in more cheerful notes, and the leaves began to bud forth on	266
the trees. Happy, happy earth! Fit habitation for gods, which, so short a time	279
before, was bleak, damp, and unwholesome. My spirits were elevated by the	292
enchanting appearance of nature; the past was blotted from my memory, the	307
present was tranquil, and the future gilded by bright rays of hope and	320
anticipations of joy."	323

Total Words Read: _____
Minus Errors: _____
CWPM: _____ _____

Name: _____ Date: _____

Chapter 13 Close Reading

"I soon perceived that although the stranger uttered articulate sounds and	11
appeared to have a language of her own, she was neither understood by nor	25
herself understood the cottagers. They made many signs which I did not	37
comprehend, but I saw that her presence diffused gladness through the	48
cottage, dispelling their sorrow as the sun dissipates the morning mists. Felix	60
seemed peculiarly happy and with smiles of delight welcomed his Arabian.	71
Agatha, the ever-gentle Agatha, kissed the hands of the lovely stranger, and	84
pointing to her brother, made signs which appeared to me to mean that he	98
had been sorrowful until she came. Some hours passed thus, while they, by	111
their countenances, expressed joy, the cause of which I did not comprehend.	123
Presently I found, by the frequent recurrence of some sound which the	135
stranger repeated after them, that she was endeavouring to learn their	146
language; and the idea instantly occurred to me that I should make use of the	161
same instructions to the same end. The stranger learned about twenty words	173
at the first lesson; most of them, indeed, were those which I had before	187
understood, but I profited by the others.	194
"As night came on, Agatha and the Arabian retired early. When they	206
separated Felix kissed the hand of the stranger and said, 'Good night sweet	219
Safie.' He sat up much longer, conversing with his father, and by the frequent	233
repetition of her name I conjectured that their lovely guest was the subject of	246
their conversation. I ardently desired to understand them, and bent every	257
faculty towards that purpose, but found it utterly impossible.	266

Total Words Read: _____

Minus Errors: _____

CWPM: _____ _____

Chapter 14 Close Reading

"Safie related that her mother was a Christian Arab, seized and made a	14
slave by the Turks; recommended by her beauty, she had won the heart of the	29
father of Safie, who married her. The young girl spoke in high and	42
enthusiastic terms of her mother, who, born in freedom, spurned the bondage	54
to which she was now reduced. She instructed her daughter in the tenets of	68
her religion and taught her to aspire to higher powers of intellect and an	82
independence of spirit forbidden to the female followers of Muhammad. This	93
lady died, but her lessons were indelibly impressed on the mind of Safie, who	107
sickened at the prospect of again returning to Asia and being immured within	120
the walls of a harem, allowed only to occupy herself with infantile	132
amusements, ill-suited to the temper of her soul, now accustomed to grand	145
ideas and a noble emulation for virtue. The prospect of marrying a Christian	158
and remaining in a country where women were allowed to take a rank in	172
society was enchanting to her.	177
"The day for the execution of the Turk was fixed, but on the night previous	192
to it he quitted his prison and before morning was distant many leagues from	206
Paris. Felix had procured passports in the name of his father, sister, and	219
himself. He had previously communicated his plan to the former, who aided	231
the deceit by quitting his house, under the pretence of a journey and	244
concealed himself, with his daughter, in an obscure part of Paris.	255

Total Words Read: _____

Minus Errors: _____

CWPM: _____ _____

Chapter 15 Close Reading

"Another circumstance strengthened and confirmed these feelings. Soon	8
after my arrival in the hovel I discovered some papers in the pocket of the	23
dress which I had taken from your laboratory. At first I had neglected them,	37
but now that I was able to decipher the characters in which they were written,	52
I began to study them with diligence. It was your journal of the four months	67
that preceded my creation. You minutely described in these papers every step	79
you took in the progress of your work; this history was mingled with accounts	93
of domestic occurrences. You doubtless recollect these papers. Here they are.	104
Everything is related in them which bears reference to my accursed origin; the	117
whole detail of that series of disgusting circumstances which produced it is set	130
in view; the minutest description of my odious and loathsome person is given,	143
in language which painted your own horrors and rendered mine indelible. I	155
sickened as I read. 'Hateful day when I received life!' I exclaimed in agony.	169
'Accursed creator! Why did you form a monster so hideous that even YOU	182
turned from me in disgust? God, in pity, made man beautiful and alluring,	194
after his own image; but my form is a filthy type of yours, more horrid even	210
from the very resemblance. Satan had his companions, fellow devils, to admire	222
and encourage him, but I am solitary and abhorred.'	231
"These were the reflections of my hours of despondency and solitude; but	243
when I contemplated the virtues of the cottagers, their amiable and benevolent	255
dispositions, I persuaded myself that when they should become acquainted	265
with my admiration of their virtues they would compassionate me and	276
overlook my personal deformity. Could they turn from their door one, however	288
monstrous, who solicited their compassion and friendship? I resolved, at least,	299
not to despair, but in every way to fit myself for an interview with them which	314
would decide my fate. I postponed this attempt for some months longer, for	327
the importance attached to its success inspired me with a dread lest I should	341
fail. Besides, I found that my understanding improved so much with every	353
day's experience that I was unwilling to commence this undertaking until a	365
few more months should have added to my sagacity.	374

Total Words Read: _____
Minus Errors: _____
CWPM: _____ _____

Name: _____ Date: _____

Chapter 16 Close Reading

"I continued for the remainder of the day in my hovel in a state of utter and	17
stupid despair. My protectors had departed and had broken the only link that	30
held me to the world. For the first time the feelings of revenge and hatred filled	46
my bosom, and I did not strive to control them, but allowing myself to be	61
borne away by the stream, I bent my mind towards injury and death. When I	76
thought of my friends, of the mild voice of De Lacey, the gentle eyes of Agatha,	91
and the exquisite beauty of the Arabian, these thoughts vanished and a gush	104
of tears somewhat soothed me. But again when I reflected that they had	117
spurned and deserted me, anger returned, a rage of anger, and unable to	130
injure anything human, I turned my fury towards inanimate objects. As night	142
advanced I placed a variety of combustibles around the cottage, and after	154
having destroyed every vestige of cultivation in the garden, I waited with forced	167
impatience until the moon had sunk to commence my operations.	177
"As the night advanced, a fierce wind arose from the woods and quickly	190
dispersed the clouds that had loitered in the heavens; the blast tore along like	207
a mighty avalanche and produced a kind of insanity in my spirits that burst	221
all bounds of reason and reflection. I lighted the dry branch of a tree and	236
danced with fury around the devoted cottage, my eyes still fixed on the	249
western horizon, the edge of which the moon nearly touched. A part of its orb	264
was at length hid, and I waved my brand; it sank, and with a loud scream I	281
fired the straw, and heath, and bushes, which I had collected. The wind	294
fanned the fire, and the cottage was quickly enveloped by the flames, which	310
clung to it and licked it with their forked and destroying tongues.	322

Total Words Read: _____
Minus Errors: _____
CWPM: _____ _____

Name: _____ Date: _____

Chapter 17 Close Reading

"I intended to reason. This passion is detrimental to me, for you do not	14
reflect that YOU are the cause of its excess. If any being felt emotions of	29
benevolence towards me, I should return them a hundred and a hundredfold;	41
for that one creature's sake I would make peace with the whole kind! But I	56
now indulge in dreams of bliss that cannot be realized. What I ask of you is	72
reasonable and moderate; I demand a creature of another sex, but as hideous	85
as myself; the gratification is small, but it is all that I can receive, and it shall	102
content me. It is true, we shall be monsters, cut off from all the world; but on	120
that account we shall be more attached to one another. Our lives will not be	135
happy, but they will be harmless and free from the misery I now feel. Oh! My	151
creator, make me happy; let me feel gratitude towards you for one benefit! Let	165
me see that I excite the sympathy of some existing thing; do not deny me my	181
request!" ...	182
His words had a strange effect upon me. I compassionated him and	194
sometimes felt a wish to console him, but when I looked upon him, when I	211
saw the filthy mass that moved and talked, my heart sickened and my feelings	225
were altered to those of horror and hatred. I tried to stifle these sensations; I	240
thought that as I could not sympathize with him, I had no right to withhold	255
from him the small portion of happiness which was yet in my power to bestow.	270

Total Words Read: _____

Minus Errors: _____

CWPM: _____ _____

Name: _____ Date: _____

Chapter 18 Close Reading

The mountains of Switzerland are more majestic and strange, but there is	12
a charm in the banks of this divine river that I never before saw equalled. Look	28
at that castle which overhangs yon precipice; and that also on the island,	41
almost concealed amongst the foliage of those lovely trees; and now that group	54
of labourers coming from among their vines; and that village half hid in the	68
recess of the mountain. Oh, surely the spirit that inhabits and guards this	81
place has a soul more in harmony with man than those who pile the glacier or	97
retire to the inaccessible peaks of the mountains of our own country." Clerval!	110
Beloved friend! Even now it delights me to record your words and to dwell on	124
the praise of which you are so eminently deserving. He was a being formed in	139
the "very poetry of nature." His wild and enthusiastic imagination was	150
chastened by the sensibility of his heart. His soul overflowed with ardent	162
affections, and his friendship was of that devoted and wondrous nature that	174
the world-minded teach us to look for only in the imagination. But even	188
human sympathies were not sufficient to satisfy his eager mind. The scenery	200
of external nature, which others regard only with admiration, he loved with	212
ardour:—	213
——The sounding cataract	216
Haunted him like a passion: the tall rock,	224
The mountain, and the deep and gloomy wood,	232
Their colours and their forms, were then to him	241
An appetite; a feeling, and a love,	248
That had no need of a remoter charm,	256
By thought supplied, or any interest	262
Unborrow'd from the eye.	266
Wordsworth's "Tintern Abbey".	269

Total Words Read: _____

Minus Errors: _____

CWPM: _____ _____

Name: _____ Date: _____

Chapter 19 Close Reading

Sometimes I could not prevail on myself to enter my laboratory for several	13
days, and at other times I toiled day and night in order to complete my work.	29
It was, indeed, a filthy process in which I was engaged. During my first	43
experiment, a kind of enthusiastic frenzy had blinded me to the horror of my	56
employment; my mind was intently fixed on the consummation of my labour,	68
and my eyes were shut to the horror of my proceedings. But now I went to it in	85
cold blood, and my heart often sickened at the work of my hands.	98
Thus situated, employed in the most detestable occupation, immersed in	108
a solitude where nothing could for an instant call my attention from the actual	122
scene in which I was engaged, my spirits became unequal; I grew restless and	136
nervous. Every moment I feared to meet my persecutor. Sometimes I sat with	149
my eyes fixed on the ground, fearing to raise them lest they should encounter	163
the object which I so much dreaded to behold. I feared to wander from the	178
sight of my fellow creatures lest when alone he should come to claim his	192
companion.	193
In the mean time I worked on, and my labour was already considerably	206
advanced. I looked towards its completion with a tremulous and eager hope,	218
which I dared not trust myself to question but which was intermixed with	231
obscure forebodings of evil that made my heart sicken in my bosom.	243

Total Words Read: _____

Minus Errors: _____

CWPM: _____ _____

Chapter 20 Close Reading

All was again silent, but his words rang in my ears. I burned with rage to	16
pursue the murderer of my peace and precipitate him into the ocean. I walked	30
up and down my room hastily and perturbed, while my imagination conjured	42
up a thousand images to torment and sting me. Why had I not followed him	57
and closed with him in mortal strife? But I had suffered him to depart, and he	73
had directed his course towards the mainland. I shuddered to think who	85
might be the next victim sacrificed to his insatiate revenge. And then I thought	99
again of his words—"I WILL BE WITH YOU ON YOUR WEDDING-NIGHT."	109
That, then, was the period fixed for the fulfilment of my destiny. In that hour I	123
should die and at once satisfy and extinguish his malice. The prospect did not	137
move me to fear; yet when I thought of my beloved Elizabeth, of her tears and	153
endless sorrow, when she should find her lover so barbarously snatched from	165
her, tears, the first I had shed for many months, streamed from my eyes, and I	181
resolved not to fall before my enemy without a bitter struggle.	192
The night passed away, and the sun rose from the ocean; my feelings	205
became calmer, if it may be called calmness when the violence of rage sinks	219
into the depths of despair. I left the house, the horrid scene of the last night's	235
contention, and walked on the beach of the sea, which I almost regarded as an	250
insuperable barrier between me and my fellow creatures; nay, a wish that	262
such should prove the fact stole across me.	270

Total Words Read: _____

Minus Errors: _____

CWPM: _____ _____

Chapter 21 Close Reading

But I was doomed to live and in two months found myself as awaking from	15
a dream, in a prison, stretched on a wretched bed, surrounded by jailers,	28
turnkeys, bolts, and all the miserable apparatus of a dungeon. It was	40
morning, I remember, when I thus awoke to understanding; I had forgotten	52
the particulars of what had happened and only felt as if some great misfortune	66
had suddenly overwhelmed me; but when I looked around and saw the barred	78
windows and the squalidness of the room in which I was, all flashed across	92
my memory and I groaned bitterly.	98
This sound disturbed an old woman who was sleeping in a chair beside	111
me. She was a hired nurse, the wife of one of the turnkeys, and her	126
countenance expressed all those bad qualities which often characterize that	137
class. The lines of her face were hard and rude, like that of persons	151
accustomed to see without sympathizing in sights of misery. Her tone	162
expressed her entire indifference; she addressed me in English, and the voice	174
struck me as one that I had heard during my sufferings. "Are you better now,	189
sir?" said she.	192
I replied in the same language, with a feeble voice, "I believe I am; but if it	209
be all true, if indeed I did not dream, I am sorry that I am still alive to feel this	229
misery and horror."	232
"For that matter," replied the old woman, "if you mean about the	244
gentleman you murdered, I believe that it were better for you if you were dead,	259
for I fancy it will go hard with you! However, that's none of my business; I am	276
sent to nurse you and get you well; I do my duty with a safe conscience; it	293
were well if everybody did the same."	300

Total Words Read: _____

Minus Errors: _____

CWPM: _____ _____

Chapter 22 Close Reading

I took the hand of Elizabeth. "You are sorrowful, my love. Ah! If you knew	15
what I have suffered and what I may yet endure, you would endeavour to let	30
me taste the quiet and freedom from despair that this one day at least permits	45
me to enjoy."	48
"Be happy, my dear Victor," replied Elizabeth; "there is, I hope, nothing to	61
distress you; and be assured that if a lively joy is not painted in my face, my	78
heart is contented. Something whispers to me not to depend too much on the	92
prospect that is opened before us, but I will not listen to such a sinister voice.	108
Observe how fast we move along and how the clouds, which sometimes	120
obscure and sometimes rise above the dome of Mont Blanc, render this scene	133
of beauty still more interesting. Look also at the innumerable fish that are	146
swimming in the clear waters, where we can distinguish every pebble that lies	159
at the bottom. What a divine day! How happy and serene all nature appears!"	173
Thus Elizabeth endeavoured to divert her thoughts and mine from all	184
reflection upon melancholy subjects. But her temper was fluctuating; joy for a	196
few instants shone in her eyes, but it continually gave place to distraction and	210
reverie.	211

Total Words Read: _____

Minus Errors: _____

CWPM: _____ _____

Name: _____ Date: _____

Chapter 23 Close Reading

She left me, and I continued some time walking up and down the	13
passages of the house and inspecting every corner that might afford a retreat	26
to my adversary. But I discovered no trace of him and was beginning to	40
conjecture that some fortunate chance had intervened to prevent the	50
execution of his menaces when suddenly I heard a shrill and dreadful scream.	63
It came from the room into which Elizabeth had retired. As I heard it, the	78
whole truth rushed into my mind, my arms dropped, the motion of every	91
muscle and fibre was suspended; I could feel the blood trickling in my veins	105
and tingling in the extremities of my limbs. This state lasted but for an	119
instant; the scream was repeated, and I rushed into the room. Great God! Why	133
did I not then expire! Why am I here to relate the destruction of the best hope	150
and the purest creature on earth? She was there, lifeless and inanimate,	162
thrown across the bed, her head hanging down and her pale and distorted	175
features half covered by her hair. Everywhere I turn I see the same figure—her	190
bloodless arms and relaxed form flung by the murderer on its bridal bier.	203
Could I behold this and live? Alas! Life is obstinate and clings closest where it	218
is most hated. For a moment only did I lose recollection; I fell senseless on the	234
ground.	235

Total Words Read: _____

Minus Errors: _____

CWPM: _____ _____

Name: _____ Date: _____

Chapter 24 Close Reading

As I still pursued my journey to the northward, the snows thickened and	13
the cold increased in a degree almost too severe to support. The peasants were	27
shut up in their hovels, and only a few of the most hardy ventured forth to	43
seize the animals whom starvation had forced from their hiding-places to seek	56
for prey. The rivers were covered with ice, and no fish could be procured; and	71
thus I was cut off from my chief article of maintenance. The triumph of my	86
enemy increased with the difficulty of my labours. One inscription that he left	99
was in these words: "Prepare! Your toils only begin; wrap yourself in furs and	113
provide food, for we shall soon enter upon a journey where your sufferings will	127
satisfy my everlasting hatred."	131
My courage and perseverance were invigorated by these scoffing words; I	142
resolved not to fail in my purpose, and calling on heaven to support me, I	157
continued with unabated fervour to traverse immense deserts, until the ocean	168
appeared at a distance and formed the utmost boundary of the horizon. Oh!	181
How unlike it was to the blue seasons of the south! Covered with ice, it was	197
only to be distinguished from land by its superior wildness and ruggedness.	209
The Greeks wept for joy when they beheld the Mediterranean from the hills of	223
Asia, and hailed with rapture the boundary of their toils. I did not weep, but I	239
knelt down and with a full heart thanked my guiding spirit for conducting me	253
in safety to the place where I hoped, notwithstanding my adversary's gibe, to	266
meet and grapple with him.	271

Total Words Read: _____

Minus Errors: _____

CWPM: _____ _____

Walton, In Continuation

"Farewell! I leave you, and in you the last of humankind whom these eyes	14
will ever behold. Farewell, Frankenstein! If thou wert yet alive and yet	26
cherished a desire of revenge against me, it would be better satiated in my life	41
than in my destruction. But it was not so; thou didst seek my extinction, that	56
I might not cause greater wretchedness; and if yet, in some mode unknown to	70
me, thou hadst not ceased to think and feel, thou wouldst not desire against	84
me a vengeance greater than that which I feel. Blasted as thou wert, my agony	99
was still superior to thine, for the bitter sting of remorse will not cease to	114
rankle in my wounds until death shall close them forever.	124
"But soon," he cried with sad and solemn enthusiasm, "I shall die, and	137
what I now feel be no longer felt. Soon these burning miseries will be extinct. I	153
shall ascend my funeral pile triumphantly and exult in the agony of the	167
torturing flames. The light of that conflagration will fade away; my ashes will	180
be swept into the sea by the winds. My spirit will sleep in peace, or if it thinks,	198
it will not surely think thus. Farewell."	205
He sprang from the cabin window as he said this, upon the ice raft which	220
lay close to the vessel. He was soon borne away by the waves and lost in	236
darkness and distance.	239

Total Words Read: _____

Minus Errors: _____

CWPM: _____ _____

Differentiated Activities
Interactive Literature Notebook
Templates

While these templates may be used for any student, they are designed to help teachers provide access to higher order thinking skills and literary analysis to struggling readers and English Language Learners.

Name: _____

Making Inferences – Chapter _____ (CCSS RL 1)

Cut out the boxes and secure them to a page in your notebook. Choose a quote from Chapter _____, write the quote under the first box, write what the passage means literally under the second box, write evidence to support your assertions under the third box, write what the passage infers under the fourth box and then write what else the passage could mean under the fifth box.

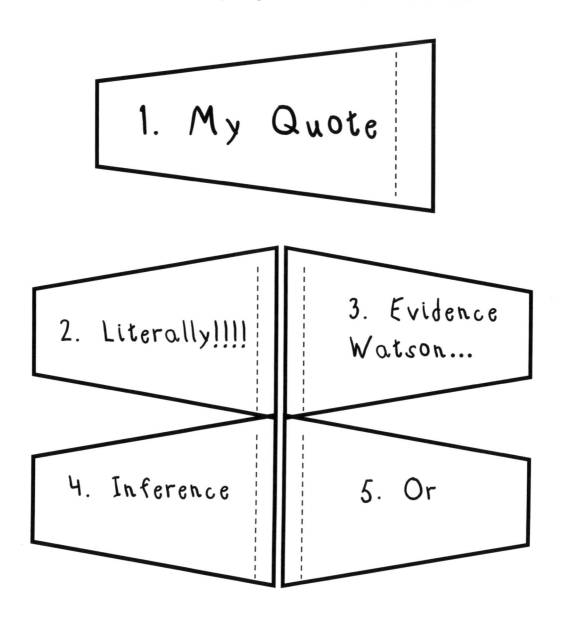

Theme – Get the Point! – (CCSS RL2)

Theme: The theme is the main idea or underlying meaning of a literary work. A theme may be stated or implied.

Cut each arrow theme out and attach them in your notebook. Note: Cut on the dashed line and fold on the solid line. Lift the arrow and write details of the theme underneath.

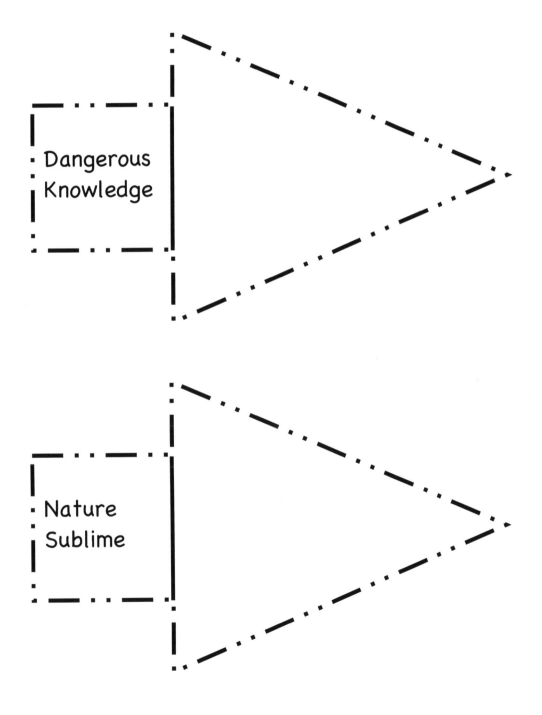

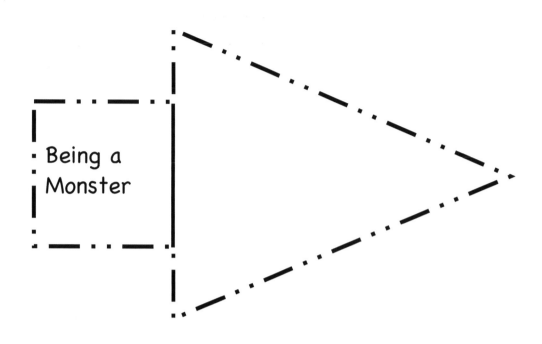

Being a
Monster

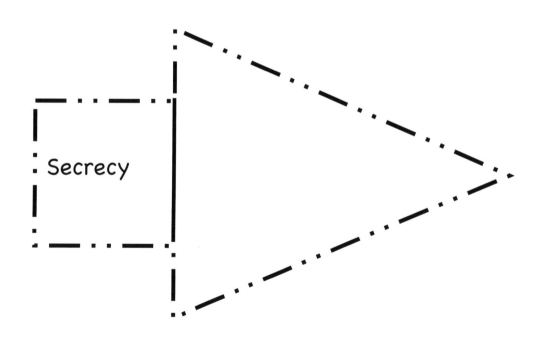

Secrecy

Themes Revisited (CCSS RL 2)

These may be cut and attached...one on top of another...in your notebook.

Attach to notebook...

Theme: Knowledge is Dangerous: At the core of Frankenstein, is the theme of the danger of the pursuit of knowledge. In fact, the thirst for knowledge proves destructive and is the center of the ultimate demise of those who seek it. **Think:** Victor's act of creation is the demise of those around him.

How is this theme introduced?	Where does it recur?	What is the culmination of this theme?

Attach to notebook...

Theme: Awesome and sublime nature: The Romantic Movement harbored the notion that nature was exalted and served as a space for spiritual rejuvenation and renewal. **Think:** Where does Victor go to feel better? What season helps the monster's heart feel light?

How is this theme introduced?	Where does it recur?	What is the culmination of this theme?

Theme: The monster within. The monster is the center of the action. The hideousness of the actual monster's physical form and the metaphorical monster of twisted personality and monstrous deeds – one who is ordinary on the outside – but consumed with hatred on the inside.

How is this theme introduced?	Where does it recur?	What is the culmination of this theme?

Theme: Secrecy: Science is a mystery whose secrets, once discovered, must be guarded. Likewise, the creation of the **monster**, as well as the actual being, must be guarded. This secrecy leads to obsession and ultimate despair.

How is this theme introduced?	Where does it recur?	What is the culmination of this theme?

Name: _____

My Frankenstein
Book Review – (CCSS RL.2)

Summary: Frankenstein is about: _____

_____

_____

_____

_____

_____

_____

_____

_____

Recommendation: _____

_____

_____

_____

_____

_____

_____

_____

_____

_____

_____

_____

_____

_____

Name: _____

Character (CCSS – RL.2)

A character is developed in four ways: physical description, what a character says, what a character does and what others say about a character.

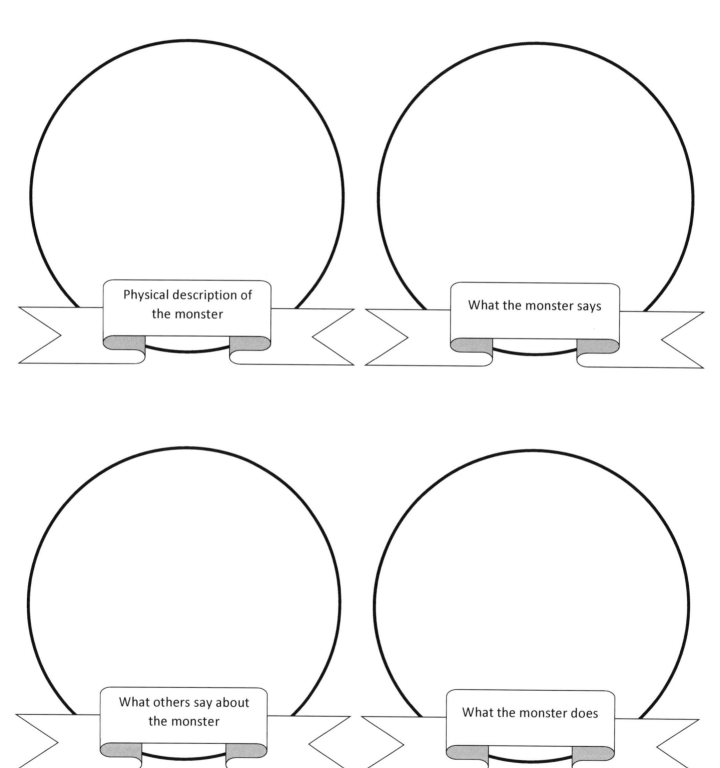

Character Traits – (CCSS RL.3)

Example

Example

Trait

Trait

Character

Trait

Trait

Example

Example

Name: _____

"Frankenstein My Way" CCSS.W.3

You are the author of Frankenstein and your publisher says you need to change the ending. Re-read the last few pages, to refresh your memory, and write another chapter...the ending after the ending. Be sure to use a lot of figurative language and creativity.

Chapter After the Novel

_____
_____
_____
_____
_____
_____
_____
_____
_____
_____
_____
_____
_____
_____
_____
_____
_____
_____
_____
_____
_____
_____
_____
_____

"Beware: for I am fearless, and therefore powerful"

Name: _____

Making Predictions (CCSS RL.2)

Instructions: Cut out the shapes below. Attach them to your notebook. At the beginning of each chapter make a prediction on the cutout. After you read the chapter, write what actually happened on the paper under the shape.

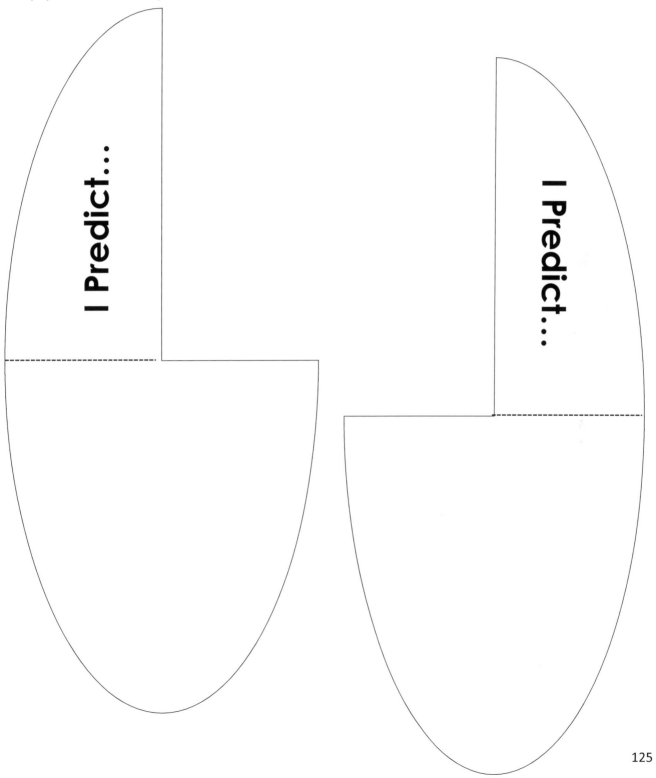

Common Core State Standards ELA 11-12
College and Career Readiness Anchor Standards for Writing

The grades 6–12 standards on the following pages define what students should understand and be able to do by the end of each grade. They correspond to the College and Career Readiness (CCR) anchor standards below by number. The CCR and grade-specific standards are necessary complements—the former providing broad standards, the latter providing additional specificity—that together define the skills and understandings that all students must demonstrate.

Text Types and Purposes
1. Write arguments to support claims in an analysis of substantive topics or texts using valid reasoning and relevant and sufficient evidence.

2. Write informative/explanatory texts to examine and convey complex ideas and information clearly and accurately through the effective selection, organization, and analysis of content.

3. Write narratives to develop real or imagined experiences or events using effective technique, well-chosen details, and well-structured event sequences.

Production and Distribution of Writing
4. Produce clear and coherent writing in which the development, organization, and style are appropriate to task, purpose, and audience.

5. Develop and strengthen writing as needed by planning, revising, editing, rewriting, or trying a new approach.

6. Use technology, including the Internet, to produce and publish writing and to interact and collaborate with others.

Research to Build and Present Knowledge
7. Conduct short as well as more sustained research projects based on focused questions, demonstrating understanding of the subject under investigation.

8. Gather relevant information from multiple print and digital sources, assess the credibility and accuracy of each source, and integrate the information while avoiding plagiarism.

9. Draw evidence from literary and or informational texts to support analysis, reflection, and research.

Range of Writing
10. Write routinely over extended time frames (time for research, reflection, and revision) and shorter time frames (a single sitting or a day or two) for a range of tasks, purposes, and audiences.

College and Career Readiness Anchor Standards
for Speaking and Listening

The grades 6–12 standards on the following pages define what students should understand and be able to do by the end of each grade. They correspond to the College and Career Readiness (CCR) anchor standards below by number. The CCR and grade-specific standards are necessary complements—the former providing broad standards, the latter providing additional specificity—that together define the skills and understandings that all students must demonstrate.

Comprehension and Collaboration

1. Prepare for and participate effectively in a range of conversations and collaborations with diverse partners, building on others' ideas and expressing their own clearly and persuasively.

2. Integrate and evaluate information presented in diverse media and formats, including visually, quantitatively, and orally.

3. Evaluate a speaker's point of view, reasoning, and use of evidence and rhetoric.

Presentation of Knowledge and Ideas

4. Present information, findings, and supporting evidence such that listeners can follow the line of reasoning and the organization, development, and style are appropriate to task, purpose, and audience.

5. Make strategic use of digital media and visual displays of data to express information and enhance understanding of presentations.

6. Adapt speech to a variety of contexts and communicative tasks, demonstrating command of formal English when indicated or appropriate.

College and Career Readiness Anchor Standards for Writing

The grades 6-12 standards on the following pages define what students should understand and be able to do by the end of each grade. They correspond to the College and Career Readiness (CCR) anchor standards below by number. The CCR and grade-specific standards are necessary complements—the former providing broad standards, the latter providing additional specificity—that together define the skills and understandings that all students must demonstrate.

Text Types and Purposes

1. Write arguments to support claims in an analysis of substantive topics or texts, using valid reasoning and relevant and sufficient evidence.

2. Write informative/explanatory texts to examine and convey complex ideas and information clearly and accurately through the effective selection, organization, and analysis of content.

3. Write narratives to develop real or imagined experiences or events using effective technique, well-chosen details, and well-structured event sequences.

Production and Distribution of Writing

4. Produce clear and coherent writing in which the development, organization, and style are appropriate to task, purpose, and audience.

5. Develop and strengthen writing as needed by planning, revising, editing, rewriting, or trying a new approach.

6. Use technology, including the Internet, to produce and publish writing and to interact and collaborate with others.

Research to Build and Present Knowledge

7. Conduct short as well as more sustained research projects based on focused questions, demonstrating understanding of the subject under investigation.

8. Gather relevant information from multiple print and digital sources, assess the credibility and accuracy of each source, and integrate the information while avoiding plagiarism.

9. Draw evidence from literary and or informational texts to support analysis, reflection, and research.

Range of Writing

10. Write routinely over extended time frames (time for research, reflection, and revision) and shorter time frames (a single sitting or a day or two) for a range of tasks, purposes, and audiences.

College and Career Readiness Anchor Standards for Reading

The grades 6–12 standards on the following pages define what students should understand and be able to do by the end of each grade. They correspond to the College and Career Readiness (CCR) anchor standards below by number. The CCR and grade-specific standards are necessary complements—the former providing broad standards, the latter providing additional specificity—that together define the skills and understandings that all students must demonstrate.

Key Ideas and Details

1. Read closely to determine what the text says explicitly and to make logical inferences from it; cite specific textual evidence when writing or speaking to support conclusions drawn from the text.

2. Determine central ideas or themes of a text and analyze their development; summarize the key supporting details and ideas.

3. Analyze how and why individuals, events, and ideas develop and interact over the course of a text.

Craft and Structure

4. Interpret words and phrases as they are used in a text, including determining technical, connotative, and figurative meanings, and analyze how specific word choices shape meaning or tone.

5. Analyze the structure of texts, including how specific sentences, paragraphs, and larger portions of the text (e.g., a section, chapter, scene, or stanza) relate to each other and the whole.

6. Assess how point of view or purpose shapes the content and style of a text.

Integration of Knowledge and Ideas

7. Integrate and evaluate content presented in diverse media and formats, including visually and quantitatively, as well as in words.

8. Delineate and evaluate the argument and specific claims in a text, including the validity of the reasoning as well as the relevance and sufficiency of the evidence.

9. Analyze how two or more texts address similar themes or topics in order to build knowledge or to compare the approaches the authors take.

Range of Reading and Level of Text Complexity

10. Read and comprehend complex literary and informational texts independently and proficiently.

Made in the USA
Columbia, SC
09 December 2019

84614816R00072